Reg Valin

Not As Planned

Recollections

Published by D&M Heritage Press
on behalf of Reg Valin

First published 2017

Text © Reg Valin

Images © Reg Valin unless otherwise attributed

ISBN: 978-1-911148-15-9

For Gitta and Claire

Acknowledgements

I would like to offer my special thanks to Richard Thoburn – the catalyst for this project – without whose enthusiastic encouragement I would not have contemplated putting these thoughts on paper.

I am also indebted to Jamie Neasham, Thoburns Creative Director, for the design and layout of the book and the presentation of the press cuttings and photographs, many of which, as a result of age, size and shape, presented him with something of a challenge. My thanks also to Sarah Minns of Thoburns for her efforts in resurrecting long forgotten cuttings from the Financial Times and Campaign archives.

I am especially grateful to my ex colleague Angus Maitland, who very kindly checked the key facts relating to the VPI years, and to Bernard Anscomb for proof reading the first draft – and discouraging the overuse of exclamation marks!

Contents

Foreword

This is primarily a personal tribute to everyone who, at one time or another, was part of Valin Pollen or, at a later stage, The VPI Group and between 1980 and 1990 helped to make it such a highly regarded company.

These were Thatcher's years and I have no doubt that we benefitted from the spirit of the age. However, I am equally certain that what we achieved, in such an extraordinarily short time, was as a direct result of the skill, professionalism, energy, creativity and immensely hard work of you all.

We had a great track record of success in competitive PR and advertising pitches – in one year winning 43 out of 47.

We also had a fine and well deserved reputation for the quality of our work and a strong commitment to client service – until events outside our control brought everything to an end.

Much of what follows, particularly in the early years, may perhaps appear mundane and trivial. However, it's a snapshot of my life – and I would like to thank each and every one of you for the crucial roles you played in what would become some of its most important years.

It was truly, for me, the best of times.

Reg Valin

Introduction

When it came, the phone call heralded the end of The VPI Group – at that time the leading financial and corporate communications company in the world.

The message was as terminal as it was clinical.

'We have no alternative but to put the company into Administration'.

Sadly, the news was not entirely unexpected since, following a raid by the Internal Revenue Service over a year earlier on the offices of our recently acquired US subsidiary, The Carter Organization, we had been battling to preserve the US business in the face of negative press comment and a steady erosion of clients.

The raid stemmed from information given to the police by the company's chauffeur when he was stopped and searched on suspicion of a drug offence. In plea bargaining, he pointed a finger at the company's accountant which then led the IRS to Don Carter, the founder of the company, who it was claimed had been overcharging his clients for expenses. It was also suggested he had avoided the payment of taxes on the cost of the refurbishment of his Park Avenue apartment by putting these through the company's books.

These problems occurred against a backdrop of a loan of $25m from Barclays and Robert Fleming a year earlier, which had been arranged to finance a stage payment to Don Carter as part of the terms of a three year 'earn out' agreement.

Subsequently, massive lawyers' costs incurred over many months, both in London and New York, together with loan interest at over 15% and a substantial reduction in US profits, all conspired to put the Group under enormous financial pressure. This led to an unsuccessful attempt by our bankers to safeguard their loans by restructuring and repositioning the Group and delisting it from the market. When it became clear that morale in the UK was also suffering as a result of the departure of key London based directors and a subsequent loss of clients, the decision was inevitable – although its impact was devastating.

It marked the end of my career in the communications industry.

* * * *

Over the years since then, I have been approached on a number of occasions with offers to write a biography about the communications company that was widely regarded as one of the Thatcher era's more visible success stories – our birth and demise coincided almost identically with those halcyon years. Until now, for a number of reasons, I have resisted – not least because I have tended to take the view that, although well known at the time, the Valin Pollen name is now long forgotten. I am also very conscious that my recollection of some of the details reflects the fact that they occurred more than 25 years ago!

However, very recently, a friend and business associate, Richard Thoburn, Chief Executive of Thoburns, with whose company and activities I have been closely involved as a consultant for the last 15 years, encouraged me to think about writing a short memoir, reflecting on some of the more important events in my business life and also my earlier background. One of his prompts was to send me a copy of Algy Cluff's memoir *Get On With It*. This struck me as excellent advice on how to live one's life and so, with some trepidation about where it will lead me, I have decided to take the plunge.

I hope one or two of my observations will touch a chord with anyone who was involved – and might be tempted to read it.

1

My Early Years

The sound of the 'Doodlebug' or 'Buzz Bomb' overhead was unmistakeable and when the engine cut I learned to count slowly to ten, awaiting the explosion.

This was one of the strongest early recollections of a very small child in London at the end of the War and, like those of other children living in the capital, it also included an unsettling mixture of daytime and night time bombing, the unmistakeable noise of anti-aircraft guns, frequent and frightening explosions and occasional glimpses of aerial combat. The roads were often littered with glass and debris whilst bomb damaged properties became a more and more common sight.

Each night I either slept under the stairs or, if I was lucky, my mother and I joined others in one of the noisy, overcrowded and unpleasant underground shelters which, oddly enough, often seemed something of an adventure.

Not As Planned

Bomb sites yielded fragments of aircraft parts, shrapnel and even empty cartridge cases as older children cycled and fought imaginary battles amid the debris, always wanting to be English – and particularly airmen – defending their small territory against the enemy.

Perhaps not the best of memories, but nonetheless an indelibly imprinted backdrop to daily life.

My early days were, otherwise, fairly unremarkable.

* * * *

Very shortly after I was born, my parents divorced – not the most auspicious of starts in life. My father was a French businessman who apparently made frequent trips abroad – I suspect he may well have had female travelling companions!

I did not meet him until I was 13.

My mother's family were from the teaching profession. My grandfather had taught maths before becoming a headmaster and my mother's elder sister taught physics – I guess it was almost inevitable that my mother would follow in the family tradition although I suspect that, once married, she had not expected to have to take up teaching again so soon, if indeed ever again.

We lived in a flat in Southfields near my grandparents and as my mother was often kept late at school attending parents' evenings, I spent quite a lot of time with them.

My grandfather sometimes taught me card games which we played for matches – possibly accounting for my subsequent predilection for gambling – and I was also encouraged to read the Encyclopaedia Britannica which I found endlessly fascinating, particularly history and information about far away places.

My grandparents also had a house on the South Coast at Lancing and I remember many long, seemingly always sunny and warm Summers, spent on the beach – swimming and shrimping in rock pools left behind by the receding tide. On some occasions my uncle, aunt and cousin, Derek Butler, who later on would have a highly successful career in property, would also be staying and this inevitably led to one of my pet hates – lengthy 'exhilarating' walks across the Downs. Although I now recognise the value of such exercise and can even be persuaded to indulge under light duress, I heartily disliked these treks and tried to make any excuse to avoid them.

In common with many youngsters, a friend encouraged me to join the Boy Scouts and endless hours were spent attempting to acquire more and more badges as well as participating in 'Bob a Job' weeks. Halcyon days, when one could call at a complete stranger's home and offer to help with domestic chores without any concerns. At about this time I was also, briefly, an enthusiastic stamp collector, but above all an avid reader, paying regular visits to the local library, particularly enjoying books about 'Biggles' by Captain W E Johns and 'Jennings' by Anthony Buckeridge.

Perhaps an even greater example of the way life and children's freedom has changed since that time, was a cycling trip I took with another school friend during the holidays at the end of my last year at Primary school. We planned a tour around Southern England, sleeping in Youth Hostels – first to Henley, on to Winchester, across to the Isle of Wight staying in Ryde and Sandown and finally back to Hindhead before returning to London. We were entirely dependent on map reading and, apart from a couple of unplanned detours, it was virtually trouble free – and quite an adventure for two 11 year olds.

In those days entertainment seemed very simple – the radio was its main source with popular comedy programmes for the family such as 'ITMA' and 'Ray's a Laugh' whilst children were glued to the set at 6.45 to listen to 'Dick Barton – Special Agent' or, a few years later, a popular Western series 'Riders of the Range.'

For children there was also Saturday Morning Cinema, frequently featuring either a comedy with Abbott & Costello or Laurel and Hardy and on occasions the indestructible cowboy Roy Rogers and his faithful horse Trigger. Wonderful escapism for children, whilst their parents did the weekend shopping.

Although rationing continued until the early 1950's, there always seemed to be plentiful supplies of milk, eggs and vegetables when I stayed at the seaside. I suspect these came from local farmers, some of whose produce may have found a way around the system.

Sweets and other exotic produce such as bananas were the last to return to the high street which may account for older people today having far fewer weight and dental problems than those who were born in the years after the War.

At that time, school class sizes would shock today's parents and teachers. I was in a class of 52 pupils when I took the Common Entrance. My mother could not afford to pay for private education on her salary, so I took an exam and won a scholarship at the age of 11 to a nearby fee paying public school – Emanuel – whose principal claim to fame at that time was that it was founded in 1594. Its quarterly magazine recently proclaimed that its notable alumni includes the founder of the worldwide web, Sir Tim Berners Lee.

Not long after starting at Emanuel, we moved near to Kingston which meant a two bus journey to get to school each morning, followed by a nearly half mile walk down the drive to arrive in time for assembly which was comprised of hymns, prayers and daily announcements. I was given quite a few detentions for lateness in the first term, simply because I was unable to rely on the times of the buses.

In my second year I was enrolled in the school Choir – but, by dint of learning to sing slightly off key, managed to avoid the Chapel Choir, whose rehearsal schedules were extremely demanding, especially ahead of the Christmas Carol Concert.

Not As Planned

Each year, the school Choir also gave a series of concerts which were very popular with parents and, I suspect, raised quite a lot of money for school funds. Most memorable among the works we performed was Handel's Messiah, which I found quite uplifting – especially the Hallelujah Chorus – which we all sang with considerable enthusiasm and inspiration.

* * * *

When I was 13 my mother told me we would be going on holiday to the South of France to meet my French grandparents. With considerable excitement, having already received the first stamp in my new passport, I boarded the train whose carriages would cross the Channel on the Night Ferry. Having been shunted from one side of Paris to the other and following a very protracted Dining Car dinner of at least 5 courses it was time to try to get some sleep in the couchette.

In the morning I peered around the blind and was dazzled by brilliant sunshine, a shimmering silver blue sea and – to the astonishment of a Londoner – palm trees, as we snaked along beside the Mediterranean, passing resort after resort all with sandy beaches, parasols and boats bobbing at anchor offshore.

When we reached Nice we were met by someone who was introduced as my uncle and we drove up into the hills high above the city to a house set amidst terraces which led down to the Var river hundreds of metres below. Having met my grandparents – my French grandfather was coincidentally a retired headmaster – I was then told that my 'uncle' was in fact my father!

In retrospect, effectively not having had a father for the first 13 years of my life, I don't recall experiencing a Damascene moment. Everything about the visit – the sunshine, the heat, the food, the architecture, the Baie des Anges, the Promenade des Anglais and the French people all made the whole experience somewhat surreal and although my father spoke perfect English and was very friendly throughout the stay, I did not feel any great sense of attachment to him.

The visit was soon over and I left not knowing if, or when, I would see him again.

As I progressed in school I eventually had to make a decision – whether to focus on Science, Arts or Classics for GCE. I found the choice difficult as I enjoyed languages but, based on exam results, was ultimately persuaded to concentrate on Science subjects. I suspect the decision was quite heavily influenced by my family's background in mathematics and sciences. I have always regretted it.

I've never been persuaded that school days are the happiest of one's life, but in the next couple of years I seem to recall finding quite a lot of time to enjoy and play Rugby, Cricket and Tennis. My mother had played a great deal of sport when she was at College and had captained the Hockey and Tennis teams, but I never showed the same aptitude for games – perhaps already exhibiting signs of Gallic genes. I do recall spending many lunch times playing Fives or Table Tennis and occasionally shooting with a .22 rifle on the school's Range, all activities which were less strenuous and certainly more relaxing than other team sports.

We had something of a reputation as a Rowing School and at around that time our First Eight won the Schools' Head of the River Race. This was a considerable achievement since it was open to schools throughout the UK. Needless to say the crew, most of whom were prefects, received a great ovation at the next day's Assembly.

Prefects were given a considerable amount of latitude in the punishment they could administer and this was still a time when corporal punishment was very common. I received my fair share of caning by teachers for minor misdemeanours but I recall, as a 14 year old, being very angry at being caned by one of the prefects. I've never understood why corporal punishment was abandoned in schools as a way of reinforcing discipline, but I do have very strong views about older boys beating younger ones.

Caning by the Headmaster in his study was something approached with trepidation and was normally accompanied by an attempt at some additional 'padding', but being caned on the hand by a master was more uncomfortable since it was particularly humiliating to have it administered in front of the class.

By now I had become a member of the school CCF, which involved a great deal of drill, but also occasional manouevres fought with thunder flashes out in the Surrey hills. There was also an opportunity to fire a more potent weapon – the .303 rifle on the range at Bisley. As soon as possible I transferred to the RAF section where the fortunate few had the opportunity to pilot a glider across the school playing fields whilst being pulled by a Jeep. I seem to recall that we never got more than about 15 feet off the ground, which was probably just as well, but it was all great fun.

* * * *

Being at a Day School, but now living some distance away from it, meant there was not a great deal of opportunity to make close school friends. I did, however, have a couple of good friends in Kingston. One, Michael Drummond, was a chorister who had such a fine singing voice that he won a choral scholarship to Cambridge a few years later. However, soon after graduating, he moved to Australia where he made a successful career in advertising. Regrettably I never saw him again. The other, John Barretto, who has been a lifelong friend, later became a Harley Street doctor.

Michael and I were keen cyclists and we both used to race each other around Richmond Park. He had a bike with no less than 8 gears, so was invariably the winner. We also used to go ice skating occasionally at Richmond Ice Rink where we briefly had illusions of becoming ice hockey players. On one occasion, cycling back alone across the park in the dark, I took a detour to save time and managed to collide with a deer – I'm not sure which of us was the more surprised, but no harm was done to either of the parties.

At about this time, Michael and I became traditional jazz enthusiasts and on Saturday evenings frequently went to the 100 Club in Oxford Street to listen to Humphrey Lyttleton. The club was especially popular among Old Etonians who flocked there to listen to a member of their alma mater and at the end of each number they would chant 'Hooray' 'Hooray'. Legend has it that the expression Hooray Henries, originally attributed to Damon Runyan, started to gain popularity as a result of Lyttleton's many enthusiastic followers. In addition to jazz, the club was one of the launching pads for many later pop groups including The Stranglers, The Sex Pistols and The Rolling Stones. The atmosphere was electric, the noise levels potentially damaging to the hearing, the buzz unbelievable and the fans good natured, mostly university students. Many of them were very attractive young women – but also very attached. At that time quite a heady mixture for a couple of first year Sixth Formers.

Meanwhile, back at school, 'A' levels were fast approaching and interviews were being arranged with the various colleges where one might hope to secure a place at University. After what I thought had been a fairly positive interview at Magdalene

College, Cambridge, I was pleased to be offered a provisional place, subject to my 'A' level grades. I was fairly optimistic about my prospects in Chemistry and Maths, although I had never felt particularly comfortable with, or enjoyed, Physics and as a result it was probably slightly neglected when the all- important revision finally started in the lead up to the exams. My recollection of revising for exams is that the process can be highly unsettling. On the one hand battling to shore up areas of weakness, whilst remaining quietly confident in other subjects where past results provided a degree of reassurance that one had a reasonable prospect of success.

The first day of the exams arrived and, as far as I could tell, all seemed to have gone reasonably well. After the first paper, the nerves were slightly less on edge, until I was confronted with my nemesis – a practical exam in Physics which, very surprisingly, featured an experiment from the 'O' level syllabus, for which I had done no revision. I made an attempt to tackle it but was sure I had failed to do justice to the question. I was pretty despondent and felt certain that the percentage of marks attributable to the experiment would have a detrimental impact on the exam result as a whole. The usual post exam analysis among friends afterwards led me to conclude that my worst fears were probably well founded. I hoped the theory paper might, nonetheless, adequately compensate for the obvious shortcomings.

Not As Planned

* * * *

A school trip to Germany had been planned for the Summer holidays and, shortly after the end of my final term, we set off for Bad Godesburg, a town on the Rhine, which was to be the first stop on our travels. The town is now part of Bonn and housed many countries' embassies. We stayed in an ancient Schloss which had been converted to provide comfortable but inexpensive student accommodation. Regrettably my strongest recollection is of a nearby bar which had a slot machine that we quickly discovered could be 'shunted' to provide a continuous payout of small denomination pfennigs!

This was intended to be a rather more cultural visit, so the following morning, in bright sunshine, we boarded a river steamer for another stage in the journey. Especially memorable en route was the Lorelei Rock, rising nearly 500 feet out of the river whose siren calls, according to legend, drew innocent sailors to their deaths. Being such an idyllic day it was difficult to attribute anything malevolent to its powerful beauty.

The next day we caught a train to Freiburg on the edge of the Black Forest. Some of our group spent a good deal of the journey in the corridor with their heads out of the window until a guard came along and shouted 'Nicht Hinauslehnen' at them. Once he disappeared, this precipitated some not entirely discreet and rather funny goose stepping along the corridor, until ugly looks from German passengers curbed their behaviour.

Once we reached Freiburg it became apparent that one of my pet hates was facing us. A trek in the Black Forest was scheduled for the next two days, before we moved on to our penultimate destination, Lindau on Lake Constance. The saving grace was an introduction to Black Forest gateau, an appreciation for which has never deserted me.

I think it would be best if I was to gloss over the details of hiking through the forest, other than to say that to me, all forests are the same and they have been left largely untouched and untroubled by humanity for very good reason.

After two or three very relaxing days by the lake, we took a train for the last, very long leg of the journey to Cologne. Here we witnessed the extraordinary renaissance and rebuilding of a city which, less than 15 years before, had been virtually flattened by massive bombing night after night by allied aircraft, but whose cathedral had continued to stand amidst the ruins, despite being badly damaged. It had now been rebuilt and stood as a beacon of hope decrying the follies of war.

A curiously poignant counterpoint to my very first memories. But now it was time to return to England – and a dramatic turn of events.

Not As Planned

2

National Service

When I arrived home I was confronted by two
life changing events. The first, but ultimately less
significant, was an envelope with my 'A' level results.
More far – reaching and dramatic was for me to
find that whilst I had been in Germany, my mother
had experienced what appeared to be some form of
mental breakdown whose effects were traumatic and
immensely painful for both of us. As a result she spent
a great deal of time in and out of hospital during the
next couple of years, whilst I had to try deal with her
personal affairs – with very little help from elsewhere.

The contents of the envelope were a shock – although
not completely a surprise. I had not attained the necessary
grade in Physics to secure the place at Magdelene. This
was well before the introduction of the Universities
Clearing System, so I no longer had a place at University.
The only option appeared to be a retake of Physics but
meanwhile, complications arose in trying to obtain
control of my mother's bank account in order to deal with

pressing bills and also in my efforts to secure a disabled teacher's pension for her. The former was far from easy and ultimately necessitated an application to the Court of Protection to authorise me, an 18 year old, to be given responsibility on a temporary basis for the management of her affairs. I was eventually able to secure the necessary authorisation and was then in a position to deal with long standing bills and various Court Summons from utilities, building societies and others to whom money had been owing for some months.

I won't dwell further on those tortuous few months, but suffice it to say it was not possible to return to school to retake my Physics paper and thus my plans to go to Cambridge were not realised. Sadly I also had to authorise electric shock treatment for my mother, against her wishes, but it worked. I have often wondered what direction my life might have taken had my original plans not been so permanently and painfully shattered – but I guess one has to adapt and 'play the game in front of you'.

I was gradually managing to create some stability in my domestic life and to help my mother to stabilise her frequently confused mental state – although at that time support systems were largely non existent – when another shock occurred in the shape of an unwelcome envelope. This contained my Call Up papers which informed me I was required to undertake military service and that I should report within the next two weeks for a medical check and an assessment.

I made representations to seek deferment on
compassionate grounds, but the claim that I was
solely responsible for my mother's wellbeing and the
maintenance of the home was totally ignored. I have
never had much faith in the State to care for the needs
of individuals, or to show real compassion or genuine
concern in dealings with them, and this incident
reinforced my conviction that from now on I would have
to fend for myself with no support from anywhere else.

Some weeks later I presented myself for a medical
examination – which unfortunately I passed with ease
– and also an assessment of my suitability for one or
other arm of the military. There had been recent press
speculation that National Service was shortly to be
scrapped and that a commission would only be possible
if one signed on for three years, so I concluded that the
Royal Air Force would be the least worst option. There
are many who have claimed that National Service was
ideal in helping to instil discipline and backbone into
young men at an impressionable age. I held a different
view both at the outset, throughout the two years and
especially after it was all over – but more of that later.

I was passed A1 and told I would receive further
instructions within the next few weeks. These duly
arrived shortly afterwards, together with a Travel
Warrant requesting me to present myself at RAF
Cardington just three days before my 19th birthday. By
no means the future I had envisaged before I left school.

Having done all I could to put things in order at home I caught an early train from King's Cross to start my two years' service in the Air Force.

* * * *

Cardington was originally acquired by Short Brothers in order to build a 700 ft hanger for the construction of the first airships the R-31 and the R-32. The hangers were extended later to provides space for the much larger and ill-fated R-101 whose tragic crash in 1930 with 40 passengers on board brought the British airship industry to a premature end. Thereafter it manufactured barrage balloons, which were used to deter German aircraft during the War, later on the RAF took it over and used it as a Reception unit for kitting out National Servicemen.

On arrival I was allocated a hut and a bed. During the day, more and more young men wandered in until by mid afternoon the room was full. Some introduced themselves to their neighbours, but most kept to themselves sitting on their beds smoking and reading. Eventually an NCO arrived and asked whether any of us had been in the CCF at school. Three hands went up including mine. On finding I had been an RAF corporal I was told 'that trumps a Lance Jack' so I was put in charge of the billet!

I soon discovered that I was meant to supervise around 20 mostly surly and resentful young men who were as enthusiastic as I was at being Called Up. A rota had to be devised to keep the bathrooms clean and the billet tidy but, as I was to learn later, this was by no means onerous by comparison with what lay ahead. Meanwhile we were provided with full RAF uniforms and all other items of kit including 'irons' – knife, fork and spoon which, we were told, must be kept safe as they would not be replaced. We were also told that in the event of their loss we would find ourselves 'put on a charge'. The significance of this remark became more apparent later when we moved on to basic training.

Towards the end of the week we were notified where we would be sent for eight weeks' basic training, which would comprise drill, fitness and weapon training, guard duty, exposure to tear gas and lectures on nuclear attack. There appeared to be some trepidation among one or two of the intake who were very anxious not to be sent to RAF Bridgenorth where it was rumoured there was a high suicide rate amongst new recruits. I was given yet another travel pass, and told to report to RAF Wilmslow in Manchester.

On arrival in Manchester I was allocated to a 'flight' and the process of training began. I was directed to a billet – 22 beds in two rows with two rectangular tables and a solid fuel stove in the middle. The floor was covered in highly polished lino which had to be kept in pristine condition, so much so that small squares torn from old blankets were piled at the entrance and on which we had to shuffle to keep the floor unmarked at all times.

Next, a ludicrously short haircut. I was put on an immediate 'charge' for suggesting how I would like it cut. We were then despatched to the parade ground where our initial drill training started. I was familiar with this from my school CCF training but that was irrelevant. We were shouted at by semi house trained NCO s whose grasp of English was limited to **** and ***** interspersed with **** and ****. Somehow we survived.

Meanwhile, we were instructed about how to lay out our kit on the bed for morning inspection. This involved a complicated presentation of every item, each of which had to conform precisely to a specified position. Morning after morning inspections were undertaken and, if not satisfactory, the contents of the bed would be thrown on the floor, sometimes with the mattress on top. Boots had to be polished till one could see one's face in them whilst canvas items, gaiters, belts and brasses were all blancoed and polished daily.

We were taught how to assemble and dismantle Bren guns and to fire them and our shooting skills were monitored on the range. There were a lot of cross country runs which were not to my taste – I used to attach myself to the end of a column of runners and as we went around the corner of one of the billets I would disappear inside. After two or three such runs I was caught and put on another 'charge' which involved reporting at the guardhouse in full, perfectly polished, kit every hour. Any small deficiency in presentation led to further returns to the guardhouse until everything was considered perfect. Another punishment involved cutting the grass outside the guardhouse with scissors or, in the event of a serious misdemeanour, a night in the cells.

The weather in March was atrocious and most of us had coughs and colds. That didn't stop us being given TABT injections for tetanus and typhoid to offer protection in the event of being given an overseas posting. We were warned in advance they would be painful – and arms swelled quite alarmingly in some cases – but I was surprised that quite a few recruits fainted once the injection had been given.

Towards the end we were tested to assess our suitability for particular 'Trades' in the next stage of training. Because of my 'A' level mathematics it was decided I should have statistics training and on passing out I was to be transferred to RAF Hereford. Before leaving Wilmslow, our flight celebrated the fact that none of our intake had committed suicide despite the abuse from sadistic drill corporals. Amidst farewells a large amount of beer was consumed – fortunately without particularly adverse after effects.

Interestingly there was little evidence of any real friendship among the members of the billet. Possibly this was as a result of widely differing social backgrounds, or perhaps because we were all, in varying degrees, fairly shocked by the malevolent behaviour of the Drill Instructors – to which we had all been continuously subjected.

Not As Planned

Service life now began to improve – especially as I was about to start my first leave.

* * * *

I was not sure what to expect, having been away for more than two months, but I hoped for the best. On arrival home I found that the situation was somewhat calmer and that my mother's medication was proving to be quite effective.

I spent a relaxing few days with friends and then left for Hereford where I was to undergo 12 weeks of further training in data processing and aircraft engine maintenance analysis. Life here was more relaxed with 48 hour weekend passes. As we were only paid a miserly £1.20 a week there was little spare money to cover train fares, so hitch hiking was the only way to get home. Getting back from Hereford to London was generally not too difficult – especially if one travelled in uniform. However, the reverse journey could be quite a problem, especially on a Sunday evening. Many an occasion I found myself in a small village on the A40 at around midnight with very little traffic and the temperature close to zero. On one particular occasion I was dropped at the bridge in Ross – on – Wye at around 1 a.m. and had to wait more than four hours before a vehicle picked me up and took me to the outskirts of Hereford. Needless to say I was late back at camp and promptly put on a charge.

It's regrettable to report that most of my spare time at Hereford was spent playing poker. My early days playing card games must have stood me in good stead since I soon became quite proficient and was able to supplement my meagre earnings with occasional winnings which were sometimes well in excess of a week's pay.

In early August I was transferred to the Headquarter of Transport Command at RAF Lyneham in Wiltshire. This was an immensely busy RAF base, with both Hercules and Comets working around the clock and transporting Army and Air Force personnel all over the world.

Not long after my posting to Lyneham, I was home on a 48 hour weekend pass when I received a telegram and Travel Warrant requesting me to return to base immediately. As soon as I got back, I was sent straight to the stores and issued with hot weather kit and very shortly afterwards I and about 20 others were taken in a coach to a Comet waiting out on the runway with its engines running. We boarded and within around 15 minutes took off. We stopped in Malta to refuel, still with no idea where we were going. Rumours started to spread that we were on our way to Aden where nearby Yemen had been stirring up trouble by fermenting fighting among local tribes.

After flying for about five hours, the plane started to shake quite violently and it dropped suddenly in what appeared to be a tropical storm. A quartermaster came through the plane and spoke to one or two of the regulars including a Flight Sergeant who was sitting alongside me. I asked him what was happening 'We're in a tropical storm and the pilot is going to try to get above it by going up to 40,000 feet.' He looked quite disconcerted and went on 'The RAF now fly the Comets which were withdrawn from service with BOAC after they started to blow up – at around 35,000 feet!' For quite a while thereafter we flew in silence, until we touched down at RAF Eastleigh in Kenya.

We disembarked and were billeted in huge hangers with row after row of beds. There appeared to be little to do except sunbathe and we were not briefed about any specific duties. However, RAF personnel were put on night guard rosters so, armed with a .303 rifle and a full magazine, I was taken out in a jeep one night to a Hercules sitting on the tarmac in the darkness and told 'Keep your eyes open otherwise you'll get a Panga in your back'. This was no idle threat as the Mau Mau insurrection was still a major problem.

My two hour stint passed uneventfully and four days later I was on my way back to Lyneham. I subsequently heard that Eastleigh was being used as a staging post for military personnel and needed temporary additional support to cope. One learned in the Forces never to ask questions.

I had made two or three applications to be moved to RAF Northolt on compassionate grounds so I could spend more time at home – I finally received authorisation early the following year. This was an ideal posting, as I was frequently able to get home in the evening, quite often on the back of a motor bike. These were the days before crash helmets and, at speeds up to 100 mph, it often felt extremely dangerous, particularly as my chum had a penchant for very fast TT style cornering. This cured me of any instinct to acquire a motor bike and I decided I would eventually have to try to save enough from my just over £2 a week to buy a car.

One or two people on the base had beaten up cars which were frequently on sale. I knew next to nothing about what went on under a car's bonnet, so I asked one of the fitters if he would give a hand. Shortly afterwards I came across what I thought was a really interesting vehicle – a 1936 Austin taxi cab. The bodywork was excellent and the interior felt as though it had been well cared for. The only drawback was that it had to be started with a starting handle, which could be a trifle temperamental! However, it had great character and once I got used to the idea of a partially open driver's cab, with the space alongside simply a platform for luggage and with a half height door, I was sold.

We agreed a price of £20 which seemed reasonably cheap, but in retrospect – ten weeks pay – was perhaps not as great a bargain as I had thought. When the weekend came, rather than the customary hair raising ride on the motor bike, I drove fairly sedately back along the A40 and parked it in the drive at home. It immediately attracted considerable attention from one or two neighbours – I suspect not all entirely favourable

– but John Barretto, who was now studying medicine at Barts, pronounced it as a beauty and immediately asked if he could borrow it to take his girlfriend out for a spin.

I was now nearing the end of what, to me, had seemed to be two years of totally wasted life. Had there been the opportunity to obtain a commission, without signing on for three years, I might have felt differently. Perhaps if I had been called upon to play a part, however small, in something of real significance I would have been much more positive about being forced to give up two years of my life. But at a time which for most young people is one of the most important stages in growing up and starting to achieve independence, I greatly resented having wasted two such valuable years.

I vowed I would ultimately find a way to make good this loss of freedom by accomplishing something worthwhile as a result of my own efforts. But, first of all, I would have to give serious thought to what I could do once I left the RAF.

A few weeks later I was given my discharge and 5011544 Reg Valin set off to explore how he might make his fortune.

3

The City Beckons

Until now I hadn't given a moment's thought to a career, since I hadn't expected to need to consider my future until after coming down from University. My family was not much help, as they all had professional backgrounds and as a result I was at something of a loss to know where to begin.

Whilst doing National Service I had corresponded occasionally with my father who had frequently offered to send me a plane ticket to join him for a holiday in Nice. I now felt a trip to the South of France would be an ideal opportunity to think about my options, so he arranged for me to join him in Nice a couple of weeks later.

When I arrived he picked me up at the airport and dropped me off at a very spacious flat on the Promenade des Anglais which apparently belonged to a business friend. It was well equipped and the fridge was stocked with a few essential supplies. He had to leave for a meeting, but we arranged to get together later for dinner in the Old Town. Meanwhile, I did some sightseeing and took a look at the beach which was crowded with parasols and highly tanned young men and women. I concluded that my ghostly pallor would not fit well amongst them and a midnight swim was my only option.

Over dinner I got to know my father a little better and we talked about his experience of working with the Americans in North Africa towards the end of the War and also his businesses in London and Nice. He suggested I should consider a business career and recommended talking to a couple of his friends in London. Over the next few days I did more sightseeing before leaving. Back in London I made a couple of calls and, following these, was much more confident about the direction I should be taking.

The advice I was given led me eventually to decide I should try to get into banking. My initial reaction had been against working in a bank since it had little appeal. However, when one of my father's friends recommended that I try to get a trainee position at one of the City banks, my mind was made up. I decided to apply to the Bank of America which at that time was the largest bank in the world. I sent a letter of Application and received a response a few days later asking me to come for an interview. I duly presented myself at their offices in Walbrook – just off Cannon Street – and shortly afterwards was invited to become a management trainee at the princely sum of £400 a year.

Meanwhile, the taxi was attracting considerable interest among my acquaintances. As a result I was frequently invited to parties – although sometimes we simply gate-crashed them. On one occasion I turned up to a rather smart town house in Chelsea, rang the bell and informed the person who opened the door, who looked somewhat older than most of my friends, that I was a friend of the owner. He informed me he was the owner and suggested in less than friendly terms that I should '**** off'! At this time, many parties in Chelsea were given by Sloane Rangers and my friend John Barretto and I would often just turn up with a bottle of wine and mingle with their Sloaney friends. We were invariably asked what we did and for a while 'fireman' or 'bus driver' never failed to elicit a great deal of amusement. One particular friend, David Hughes, who was a naval diver, was simply unable to persuade the girls of his real identity.

That Summer, John Barretto and I managed to watch some great tennis at Wimbledon, with players like Lew Hoad, Rod Laver and Ken Rosewall dominating the men's game. By comparison with the much improved standard of women players today, I suspect Serena Williams might even have been quite a tough opponent, but their artistry and touch was of the finest order.

At the bank I was spending a month or two with different departments – Foreign Exchange, Remittances, Trade Finance, Securities etc. It was far from challenging and there was little scope to exercise initiative or to interact with clients. Although feeling somewhat disillusioned, I had only been at the bank five months so I concluded I would have to stick it out for a while longer.

Having heard about my taxi, one or two of my colleagues asked whether they could see it. I drove it up to work one morning and parked it in Walbrook amidst curious stares. Not quite what the City was accustomed to seeing – although a number of black cab drivers seemed very enthusiastic about it. At the end of the day a group of seven or eight of us piled in and we set off to the West End. Unfortunately, as I was driving up The Mall, towards Buckingham Palace, someone called out to me through the sliding window behind my head. I turned slightly and must have pulled the wheel a little to the right as the next moment I hit the base of a traffic island only about 50 or 60 yards from the Palace. Those in the back were thrown around and one or two things fell onto the road which then caused a traffic jam and brought us to the attention of the police. Fortunately nobody was hurt and everyone, apart from the police, thought it was incredibly funny. Sadly the taxi had a buckled front wheel and could not be moved, but eventually a breakdown vehicle arrived and it was taken to a garage in Soho to be repaired.

However, to adapt John Cleese's immortal words 'this was a dead taxi'! The vehicle was pronounced beyond repair as a result of the buckled wheel for which there was no possibility of finding a replacement in view of the vehicle's venerable age. There was thus no alternative but to get it scrapped however, before doing so, I had to organise a tow. Fortunately another friend, Tony Beavis, whose company now supplies cables to some of the world's largest power companies, had a jeep and a length of cable which we used to tow the taxi back to Kingston. The sight of the two vehicles driving through the streets caused a good deal of amusement, and even some clapping, which seemed appropriate for the demise of such a distinctive and much loved vehicle.

* * * *

I had now been at the bank for six months and was entitled to a week's holiday. John Barretto, still an impoverished trainee doctor, suggested we should hitch hike to Paris where another mutual friend was living. We left London reasonably early and made good progress towards Dover to catch the ferry, when John suddenly told me he had only £4 with him! This did not augur well for our further progress. However, his girl friend was on holiday with her family in Rye and was prevailed upon to drive over to meet us in Dover with some additional cash. With raised spirits we caught the next ferry and were soon in France.

It took a while to get out of Calais, by which time we were feeling pretty tired. We managed to get one lift in the direction of Paris but ended up in a small village just as it was beginning to get dark. There appeared to no option but to sleep in a haystack which proved to be reasonably comfortable, albeit a trifle chilly, but the absence of washing and showering facilities had taken their toll and we both looked pretty dishevelled in the morning. We therefore reluctantly concluded that we would have to settle for a day trip to France and get back to England. I guess we should have been better prepared and resourced and with a clearer idea of our objectives – maybe if we'd had John's girlfriend with us it would have helped, with the classic ploy of the distressed female stopping the vehicle and the guys leaping out from behind a hedge.

I hadn't bothered to shave whilst away, nor immediately on my return. A couple of days later I went to a party being given by a model agency. While I was standing nursing a drink, looking around the room and listening to the music I noticed a very pretty girl standing rather shyly on her own. I went over to introduce myself – this time not as a fireman and apologising for my unshaven appearance – and asked whether I could get her a drink. She told me she didn't drink, so I offered a glass of milk which I managed to get from the fridge. We talked for quite a while and she told me she was born in Silesia and her name was Brigitte or 'Gitta'. She was the PA to the Managing Director of a mining engineering company with operations in the Saar and had apparently only been living in London for two months. After a while she said she had to leave to meet someone and, somewhat to my surprise in view of my unshaven appearance, she agreed to let me drop her off at the tube. Before we parted I managed to get her telephone number.

Can you tell where this might be going?

A couple of days later I called the number, which I discovered was that of the Helena Ladies Club in Lancaster Gate and arranged to meet her for coffee. On the chosen day I rang the doorbell of what appeared to be a private hotel and was shown into a large lounge overlooking Hyde Park. A number of young women were sitting there chatting or reading magazines – I was disconcertingly and very conspicuously the only male. Gitta turned up after a few minutes and once we left she told me it was a standard ritual for new young men to be looked over by the other girls – I guess I got through the first interview because she did agree see me again.

Being just opposite the Park, in the early days of our relationship we often walked across to the Albert Hall, where we occasionally attended concerts, whilst a great deal of time was also spent in coffee bars deep in conversation about art, films and literature – it's a wonderful thing to be young and in love.

* * * *

At the bank there were a couple of very pleasant social occasions, firstly the annual Christmas Party, for which Gitta joined me – at the time I felt this was a promising sign – and a then a splendid and very dramatic performance of Boris Godunov at the

Royal Opera House which Gitta also attended. My modest salary would not have normally covered such an expense but the bank had an arrangement with Covent Garden whereby staff had access to heavily discounted tickets, which were naturally in great demand and much appreciated.

Early in the New Year, I decided to leave the bank as it was clear I was totally unsuited to its very structured working practices, which reminded me far too much of my time spent in the RAF. I wanted to stay in the City but felt that a role with greater personal responsibility and accountability would be better suited to my temperament and personality. Not long after this, I saw a job being advertised for an account executive with City experience to work for a City based advertising agency. I wrote giving some background about my current responsibilities and was pleased to be asked to attend an interview with a company called Charles Barker which had offices in Watling Street just behind St Paul's Cathedral.

Some research revealed an apocryphal story about the original Charles Barker. Seemingly he had been a London Times correspondent at the Battle of Waterloo and with considerable foresight had realised that the Duke of Wellington's forces were about to emerge victorious. He rushed to the coast and managed to get the last steamer back to England whereupon he went straight to Rothschild's office to tell them the good news. With the benefit of this information, they made a great deal of money trading in Government Bonds, and Charles Barker was rewarded with their advertising business. Rather interestingly I also discovered that their current Chairman, Gerald Wellesley, was one of the Iron Duke's descendants.

A few days later I went for an interview with two of the company's directors, Peter Spencer-Smith and Kyrle Simond. The former, the Managing Director and an Old Etonian. Kyrle Simond, I later discovered, was reputed to have been the youngest Colonel in the British Army during the War. They were an impressive pair. Both tall, stylish and charming, although their questioning was sharply focused. When the interview was over, the MD walked with me to the lift and in a slightly jocular manner drew attention to a slight smear of lipstick at the bottom of my cheek where Gitta had given me a good luck kiss earlier. Somehow I thought that might be a good omen.

Shortly afterwards and to my great pleasure, I received a letter thanking me for my attendance at the interview and asking me to join the company as an account executive at a starting salary of £480 p.a. – with a review after a further three months.

I accepted with alacrity and also considerable relief and gave the bank immediate notice. It was agreed that I would start with Charles Barker after Easter.

At last I sensed that I was at the beginning of an exciting new career with great opportunities – it was not to disappoint me.

Not As Planned

4

Charles Barker

My new job was to plan and manage advertising campaigns for public companies in the financial and business pages of the press. It also involved issuing press releases for companies that did not retain a PR consultancy. The advertising was largely based on information drawn from the client's Annual Report and its purpose was to highlight their financial performance – thus stimulating interest in the company as a potential investment. In some respects the precursor of today's investor relations.

On my third day, my boss asked me join him for what he described as a meeting of enormous significance. This took place at the offices of Phillip Hill, Higginson, Erlanger's – one of the City's Merchant Banks, who later merged with M Samuel to create Hill Samuel. Leo d'Erlanger was to give a press conference accompanied by key people from the Channel Tunnel Study Group. As the Study Group had no PR budget, but the bank was a Charles Barker client, we had been asked to assist them in dealing with the press. The presentation was impressive and outlined the work that had been undertaken to assess the feasibility of a tunnel under the Channel. I was left in no doubt that the project had every prospect of succeeding if the necessary funds could ultimately be raised. I was so impressed I decided that, if an opportunity ever presented itself, I would invest in the company and try to be a passenger on the first train journey to Paris. More of that later.

Meanwhile, I was working on proposals for clients, putting together media recommendations and briefing creative people to prepare visuals for client presentations. Media planning specialists did not exist in those days which meant I had regular contact with advertising executives in papers such as the FT, The Times, Daily Telegraph and Sunday broadsheets as well as The Economist and Investor's Chronicle. These individuals seemed to have very sizeable expense accounts and were tasked with securing advertising for their papers. The inevitable result was that I now found myself being lunched quite frequently and lavishly in some of the West End's best restaurants! I pointed out that planning decisions were based both on budget and target audience – either institutional, intermediary or private – and that readership figures were not always the sole factor in making media decisions, but the lunch invitations kept coming. I suspect some of them may have simply wanted to produce reports showing evidence of activity.

At about this time Gitta and I were thinking about becoming engaged, so I felt it might be an appropriate moment to discuss my career prospects. I mentioned this to my department head who referred the matter to Peter Spencer- Smith with whom, shortly thereafter, I had a very positive conversation and was given a very welcome salary increase.

However, not everything was smooth sailing. I worked on some major client projects where one or other of the directors had ultimate responsibility. One such, involved Kryle Simond who looked after financial advertising for Mitchells & Butlers, the Birmingham brewery. I was asked to prepare three alternative media proposals at different budget levels which Kyrle forwarded to the company. The next day I was summoned to his office – he handed me the plans and asked me to tell him what was wrong with them.

Since I was unable to see an error, he drew my attention to the totals which had been transposed when being typed. Kyrle told me the Chairman of the company would be in his office the following day and that I should be ready to make a personal apology and explain the reason for my mistake. This I did, but the Chairman couldn't have been more understanding – however, I quickly learned just how tough a task master Kyrle could be if work was not perfect.

I took that lesson to heart and never forgot it, as I think it's one of the small but key tenets of business success. In planning anything important it's a good maxim to always check and double check everything to avert any possibility of Sod's Law.

* * * *

Meanwhile Gitta and I got married and moved into a modest one bedroom flat in Highgate. Not an area with which I was familiar, but despite both of us working it was all we could afford at the time. We spent our honeymoon in the South of France where my father put a house at our disposal. However, after a few days we were joined unexpectedly by John Barretto who was nearby and felt we might get bored if we were left alone too long!

When we returned to London we agreed that, once funds permitted, our priority would be to try to find a flat in Kensington rather closer to most of our friends. We were quite fortunate when, towards the end of the year, we were able to move to a larger flat in Holland Park. The following year, our daughter, Claire, was born in nearby St Mary Abbot's Hospital. Sadly, very shortly after this my father died unexpectedly – regrettably, I hardly knew him and he never knew Claire.

At around this time, Charles Barker were asked to help with a major Government project – the denationalisation of the steel industry which featured pages and pages of prospectuses published in the national press, giving details of the operations of more than a dozen steel companies. This was a mammoth task and many of us were involved in checking to ensure every detail within the advertisements was correct. I suspect it also had a fairly dramatic impact on Charles Barker's bottom line as, not long afterwards, the company moved to a larger new office development at 20 Cannon Street, immediately next door to Bracken House, then the HQ of the Financial Times. This building provided much more spacious accommodation with meeting and lunch rooms as well as a small cinema in which clients could be shown commercials or rough cuts of corporate films.

I had now become an account director with responsibility for a number of major financial marketing clients including M&G Group, Midland Bank and Merrill Lynch – my team included an account executive, an executive assistant and a secretary/PA.

One morning I found a note on my desk from my secretary who had been offered a better paid job elsewhere. She had been with me for around 18 months and I didn't look forward to finding a replacement. However, after three or four unsatisfactory interviews the recruitment agency proposed that I meet a young lady called Baroness Marie Christine von Reibnitz. I was impressed by her enthusiasm and desire to work in an advertising agency but, as it was apparent she had a fairly active social life, I warned her that departure at 5.30 in the evening might not always be feasible. This did not seem to be a deterrent and she joined a couple of weeks later.

Marie Christine had a relaxed and charming manner and was both energetic and resourceful. She had a particularly engaging way of addressing very senior clients by their Christian names which, although a trifle unorthodox, never seemed to cause a problem. She apparently also knew one or two of the Charles Barker Group Board socially and at our Annual Dinner asked me to introduce her to Peter Spencer – Smith who was now the company's Chairman. I took her over to meet him and, having talked together for a few minutes, she said 'Reg works so hard, is he soon going to become a director?' I felt it wise to keep a discreet distance from him for the rest of the evening!

There was a certain inevitability about her departure. As I envisaged, a constant round of dinner parties was not compatible with the demands of a fairly pressurised adman's needs and after about four months we both agreed it would be for the best if she pursued an entirely different career which, of course, she did later with customary verve and flair as a member of the Royal Family.

The Merrill Lynch business continued to increase as they opened offices throughout Europe and we ran advertising campaigns in support of them. These campaigns were an important component of their global expansion programme and their Chief Executive and the International Marketing Director regularly came over to London for a presentation of our proposed programme for the next 12 months. After one such meeting, drinks were proposed and both of the Americans asked for a Martini. I was deputed to act as bartender and mixed what I considered to be a decent Martini – 5 or 6 parts of gin with one of vermouth, ice and a twist of lemon, all well shaken. I poured the Martini into two glasses, each with an olive and passed them to our guests hoping they would be to their taste. The CEO took a sip and spat it back in the glass. ' What the hell is that' he snorted. Having explained, he asked me to shake up some more gin with ice – he then put one drop of the drink I'd originally prepared into the glass and pronounced 'That's a Martini'. Mercifully this episode did not have a detrimental effect on our longer term business relationship.

At around this time a tricky event arose with one of my other clients. I was asked to attend a meeting with a director from Hambros and was introduced to a South African businessman, Mark Weinberg, who had launched a unit linked insurance product and now wished to market it. An advertisement was hastily prepared and appeared in the weekend's papers. On the following Monday morning, John Fairbairn, the Marketing Director of M & G, called me with a request to find out about the newcomer and who had placed the advertising. I was extremely discomfited to have to explain it was me. He made it plain it was not to be repeated if we wished to retain M&G's business.

Not As Planned

There had been talk for some time of a shake up in the banking system and the launch of a national Girobank for those without bank accounts. The British Clearing Banks – then 16 in all – were concerned about the implications of this perceived threat to their business and asked Charles Barker to develop a campaign to counteract it. After extensive research, a number of commercials were developed by Jean Wadlow, Charles Barker's Head of Film and Television, with the theme of 'The Bank Manager in the Cupboard' the objective being to personalise banking by bringing a friendly bank manager directly into the home . These were initially presented to all 16 Assistant General Managers, then to the General Managers and finally to the Chief General Managers at their Head Office in 10 Lombard Street. We had been warned that many of the CGMs didn't watch much TV, so individual monitors were put in front of each of them and our commercials were included among other current big brand advertisers to create a feeling for the environment within which they would be appearing. At the end of the presentation, Len Mather, Midland's CGM turned to his colleagues to express satisfaction with the campaign, upon which two of them admitted to never having seen a TV commercial before! Shortly after this, Jean also produced a brilliant animated commercial for my client Midland Bank, which won a much coveted Grand Prix and a number of other international industry Awards.

I was now an Associate Director and fortunate to work with some versatile, but occasionally temperamental, creative people. One, with whom I am still in contact, was Peter Cruikshank, a Canadian who had lived in London for some years and was one of the agency's Creative Group Heads. He eventually left Charles Barker and returned to his home city, Vancouver, where he is now a very successful property developer. Another, James Herbert, sadly now no longer with us, was an Art Director and Creative Group Head on a number of my accounts. Jim did not appreciate his work being rejected. More than once he told me not to bring it back if the client wasn't satisfied. Jim became famous for his horror stories, many of which were made into films and latterly enjoyed the reputation of being a home grown Stephen King.

Gitta and I were never great beach holiday or Summer resort enthusiasts, although we both enjoyed skiing. Over the years we took a number of skiing holidays with friends in either Austria or Switzerland. On one occasion we were in a villa party in Klosters when, for 10 days, it snowed so heavily all the ski lifts were closed. We were fortunate to have Norris McWhirter of the Guinness Book of Records fame in the party – one of his many tricks was tearing a telephone directory in half. Very sadly his twin brother was murdered by the IRA some years later.

On another occasion, in Zermatt. I was skiing alone, and too fast, which led to a very heavy fall and a deep gash just under my knee, caused by the edge of the ski. I had to be stitched up in the local clinic, but thought it best to adopt the 'get straight back on the horse' principle, so immediately went up for another run. By now the leg was quite stiff, but I was none the worse for the experience, apart from the fact that the mountain was virtually deserted and it was almost dark when I finally got down – perhaps not such a great idea.

* * * *

As part of our career development, Associate Directors and Account Group Heads were occasionally subjected to personal development programmes. These included familiarising oneself with the principles of Management by Objectives which had become very fashionable and also Public Speaking training. One of these sessions involved picking up a postcard from a table and then talking to one's peers and sometimes Group Board directors for 5 minutes about whatever was the topic on the card. Another test of confidence – or nerves – was TV training. We offered this service to Chairmen and Chief Executives of client companies, so it was thought desirable that we should be put through the process ourselves. I well remember being questioned on camera by a well known TV personality who told me he would start with some easy questions before becoming more forceful. On playback all seemed to be going reasonably well until I was subjected to a hostile barrage at which stage he drew my attention to the increasingly firm grip I was exerting on the sides of the chair. Apart from this, he seemed to think the session had gone reasonably well, but he emphasised the importance of remaining calm and reassuring and never allowing oneself to get heated or aggressive by a hostile interviewer.

Shortly after this, I had a career review with Kyrle Simond who asked me if I would be prepared to take over responsibility for running the advertising division of one of the Group's newer subsidiaries, Charles Barker City. At that time the company was quite small – no more than a couple of dozen people of which the advertising division numbered rather less than half. I had some reservations, but on being told I would be appointed a director of CBC and would have a car and a parking space in the company's garage – thus no more tube journeys – the decision was clear. I accepted with alacrity, but I did have some concerns about the lack of creative resources in the new company. I didn't realise it then, but this was to become my preparation for a very much bigger goal.

Not As Planned

5

Charles Barker City

At that time, CBC was primarily a financial PR company, headed by George Pulay, who previously had been the first Business Editor of The Times. Its office was at the back of the FT building in Queen Victoria Street. The Daily Telegraph's City office, headed by Business Editor Andreas Whittam Smith, who subsequently helped to found and then became the first editor of The Independent, was also conveniently located in the same part of the building.

It was immediately apparent that CBC had far too many small clients – over 200 – who made a negligible contribution to overheads and required a disproportionate amount of servicing. I discussed this with Kyrle Simond and proposed writing to all of them to introduce myself and explain that a fee arrangement would have to be introduced immediately, to cover the cost of basic press release services, notwithstanding the level of their advertising expenditure.

This had an immediate effect. CBC lost nearly 60% of its small clients, but the additional income from new fees more than covered the income lost and produced sufficient revenue to cover the cost of hiring our own creative team, rather than having to rely on services provided by the parent company in the building next door.

I think I probably ruffled some feathers, as my arrival coincided with the departure of two senior people, one of whom moved to Dewe Rogerson where he later joined the Board – the other set up his own company.

My early priority was to improve the quality of the team with talented and resourceful people, to do better work for our clients, to foster pride in our division within CBC and to seek to make it the most profitable part of the company. After a short time we were able to recruit an excellent Art Director and not long afterwards an extremely talented and versatile Copywriter, Chris Greening, with whom I was to work closely for many years. So now we were much better resourced.

CBC's advertising clients were mostly extremely conservative and reluctant to run any advertising which could be construed as being 'adventurous.' One of our clients was Spillers, the flour manufacturers who had developed the cartoon 'Flour Graders ' for their TV ads. We attempted to persuade them to use these characters in their corporate style ads – but unfortunately their consumer agency objected.

We were now developing much higher quality creative work and, little by little, imaginative headlines, stronger visuals and powerful graphics were becoming more acceptable among hitherto conservative clients.

In an effort to encourage financial/corporate advertisers to be more creative, The Times introduced an Award Scheme for the best Financial Advertisement of the Year.

CBC won a Gold Award in the first year of the scheme and were to become the most successful agency in regularly winning such awards for our creative work. Awards were incredibly good for morale and I constantly encouraged my colleagues to produce award winning campaigns.

I was anxious to gain introductions to the clients of CBC's PR division, although I found this quite difficult as PR people often consider public relations to be a far more effective communications weapon than advertising. This is, of course, a fallacy since there are many occasions when a targeted advertising message to a precisely defined audience can be more effective than a diffuse one – however independent the editorial source may be. Advertising and PR complement each other as key parts of an overall marketing and communications mix, and each has its own role and relevance, depending on the requirements of the brief.

* * * *

Our parent company had acquired a small stake in a PR company, John Addey Associates, which was run by the eponymous John Addey. Not long after this, one of John's clients, Debenhams, was on the receiving end of an unwelcome bid from United Drapery Stores, which the Chairman of Debenhams, Sir Antony Burney, forcefully rejected. Sir Anthony Burney had a twin approach to fighting UDS – keep the initiative and ensure shareholders were fully briefed. I was asked to work with John in developing marketing ideas in support of his PR activity, so in order to inject more originality into the campaign, CBC created posters for 100 Debenhams stores, carrier bags for customers with 'Hands Off Debenhams' slogans and finally we were able to persuade Sir Anthony to make a record to be sent to every shareholder explaining why Debenhams should remain independent. This was the first time such a tactic had been used in a takeover battle and it proved to be highly effective. At the conclusion of what had been a long and very hard fought campaign, Sir Anthony finally won convincingly and Debenhams remained an independent company.

Meanwhile we moved yet again and all companies within the Charles Barker Group were finally reunited in a large building in Farringdon Street. CBC occupied the whole of the first floor with the PR division on the floor above. It was now agreed that the two divisions should become separate profit centres which made it easier for me to remunerate people based on their individual performance, rather than on a notional assessment of each division's profitability.

CBC was continuing to grow quickly and I had hired a sufficient number of people including Simon Dixon and Peter Rees to be able to introduce an Account Group system, which helped to foster a greater competitive instinct among the newer Group Heads. We continued to experiment with original ideas and when Pilkington, the glass manufacturers, floated on the Stock Market we were able to persuade them to run what was to be the first ever colour Prospectus to be published in the FT. More corporate advertising in colour followed, with an outstanding campaign for the French company Saint- Gobain following its merger with Pont-a-Mousson.

It was clear that CBC required a stronger media planning and buying system and we decided to hire a media manager to take overall responsibility for the Media function. Sadly the person we recruited died very shortly after joining us. Ultimately we were fortunate to be able to recruit John Hall from our sister company's Media Department.

The Group now acquired another PR company – FJ Lyons – which was merged with CBC's PR division to create a new company, Charles Barker Lyons. This meant that Charles Barker City was now a fully independent subsidiary within the Group and I was appointed its Managing Director.

Not long after this, I recruited someone who was to play a very significant part in my future business life. Richard Pollen had been a very successful marketing executive at the FT and we had enjoyed a number of interesting discussions about the importance of corporate communications in helping companies to raise their profile among audiences ranging from shareholders and intermediaries to customers and opinion formers. I offered Richard a job with CBC and was delighted when he accepted, as he had immense enthusiasm and energy and exceptional business development talents.

Now, a rather amusing incident occurred. The media were always looking for new ways to encourage advertisers to use colour and Euromoney – which carried a great deal of 'Tombstone' advertising featuring lists of banks who participated in syndicated loans – ran a dummy colour advertisement in the magazine with a number of fictitious names. These included such well known City institutions as Sue, Grabbit & Run and The First City Bank of Boot Hill etc. After the advertisement appeared I received a call from the London Manager of a small Japanese Bank to enquire why their bank had not been invited to participate in this lending syndicate. The conversation that followed stretched all my diplomacy skills to the limit.

We were still experimenting with new approaches to communicating with shareholders and started to discuss with London Weekend Television whether it might, for the first time, be possible to advertise a company's financial results on TV within the framework of the constraints imposed by the rules governing the advertising of financial information. We were eventually able to persuade Glynwed, the makers of Aga and Rayburn cookers, that television would be a good medium since not only would it reach an investment audience, but could also showcase their range of cookers. We developed a creative treatment and, as an investment in what they hoped might be a new source of advertising revenue, LWT handled the production. After the commercial had aired, Glynwed's Chairman, Sir Leslie Fletcher, joined Richard Pollen and me and the LWT team for a celebratory dinner at Le Gavroche and pronounced his considerable satisfaction with what had been accomplished – another first for CBC. The evening was very slightly marred by the fact that the restaurant did not accept credit cards and neither Richard nor I had a cheque book with us!

Through the personal connections of Anthony Snow, one of the Group Board's directors, an opportunity arose for me to present advertising proposals to the South African mining groups De Beers and Anglo American. Having won the business, I went out to South Africa with Don Kennedy, the Account Director, to meet members of the board and senior management and to develop our ideas. This was a fascinating trip, at one stage involving a descent into the Rustenberg mine, which gave a very sanitised idea of what working deep underground must have been like for African workers. This was still the time of Apartheid and we had an uncomfortable feeling about the prevailing atmosphere. At night there were hardly any black Africans around, apart from those working in the Carlton Hotel where we were staying, as they had to return to Soweto to conform with Government Regulations. It felt as though we were sitting on a time bomb and it might not be long before things would ultimately explode.

* * * *

I had now become Chief Executive of CBC and been appointed to the Group Board. CBC had continued to grow rapidly and was one of the Charles Barker Group's largest profit contributors. Kyrle Simond had retired as Chairman and Julian Wellesley, whose father had been Chairman when I first joined the company, now took over. That Summer, I attended a weekend seminar for Group Board Directors at which we were to discuss strategy and business development. I put forward a number of ideas for developing the corporate business of CBC, including the possibility of taking a strategic stake in a specialist design company, Michael Peters and Partners – who had a reputation for top flight corporate design. I also wanted to explore the possibility of building the CBC 'brand' in other financial centres but the Group's emphasis was on its consumer agency, which had recently started to build a network to rival JWT, Ogilvy, Saatchi etc. I also questioned the current situation whereby the directors only held a very small stake in what was a private company and whether more shares, currently held by two Merchant Banks, Barings and Schroders, could be made available to those who were responsible for generating the Group's profits. I was told quite emphatically by two of the more senior directors that such a proposal was unlikely to be acceptable and not to pursue it.

For the first time since joining Charles Barker, I began to feel I had perhaps reached a ceiling in my career with the company.

CBC was beginning to gain a higher profile in Campaign, the advertising industry's trade paper and was finally winning more projects from Charles Barker Lyons. As a result of CBL's work on behalf of clients who were alarmed at the possible implications of future Labour Party policies, we had the opportunity to develop two very interesting political campaigns. The first of these was called 'Patients before Politics' and, backed by BUPA and other medical insurers, highlighted the potential dangers of greater interference in the private sector by the Labour Government.

Another controversial campaign was created at very short notice for Amoco, the US oil company. Amoco, in common with a number of North Sea oil operators was concerned about the threat of a Petroleum Revenue Tax being introduced by the Government and we were briefed to develop a series of advertisements to present the case against such a measure. It was put together at great speed and I had to fly to Milan early on Boxing Day morning to present our ideas. I spent the day in a basement meeting room before leaving after dark to return to London – I barely saw Milan in daylight.

I first met Stuart Fenwick, then with LWT, at a Marketing Society Conference in Eastbourne, where I was scheduled to speak about corporate communications. On the same platform was Anthony Wreford, the FTs marketing manager who was to address the subject from the media perspective. Stuart's role was to ensure that all of the visual material and films were precisely synchronised with our talks and that everything went off smoothly. I was to get to know each of them very much better a few years later.

For quite some time I had been concerned that our ability to contribute to the planning process in developing campaign strategy was being diminished by the absence of a Planning capability and decided this now needed to be urgently rectified. We placed an advertisement in The Economist and received well over 100 replies. I decided to interview half a dozen of the respondents including Angus Maitland, an economist with the Weir Group in Scotland. I was enormously impressed by his quietly confident and authoritative demeanour, his obvious professionalism and his formidable intellect. We agreed he would join us as soon as he could move down to London. Angus would play a pivotal role in everything that was to follow later.

Charles Barker City

Charles Barker had formed an alliance with the American advertising agency NW Ayer in order to jointly promote global brands. Shortly after this I went to New York to assess the possibility of building financial and corporate advertising opportunities between out two companies. This led to the creation of Charles Barker Ayer Financial with whom we eventually collaborated on one or two projects.

While in New York, I always made a point of meeting influential US business media – especially The Wall Street Journal and the Institutional Investor who were both useful potential sources of business introductions. I had maintained a close relationship with the latter, whose marketing people – especially Arnie Obler and Fred Rubinstein – were regular visitors to CBC, together with Christine Cavolina who headed up their UK operations. Their founder, Gil Kaplan, was a Mahler aficionado and after receiving expert training, conducted Mahler's Second Symphony more than 100 times, on one occasion at the Royal Festival Hall, to which he very kindly extended an invitation.

* * * *

Following a particularly protracted review meeting with Dick Law, the head of communications at Hawker Siddeley, which was attended by eight Charles Barker people, I was asked why it was necessary to field 'a football team.' I explained the roles of the different specialists – PR, Government Relations, Film, Account

Management, Media Planning, Creative etc. – but after the meeting Dick asked for a private word. He told me he didn't appreciate having to pay for the time of so many people and would prefer to deal with me alone. I explained that Charles Barker was not structured to provide a single point of access to all services, whereupon he suggested that I start to think about getting the system changed.

From time to time I had talked to Richard Pollen, now an Assistant Managing Director, about the possibility of setting up a new corporate communications consultancy along the lines suggested by Hawker Siddeley. In this we were greatly helped by Jean Wadlow, who for a couple of years had been running her own film production company, Wadlow Grosvenor. Jean, who has been a good friend for many years, very kindly acted as the 'midwife' to our plans by hosting two or three suppers at her flat which finally led me to decide I would resign, once I returned from a Spring skiing holiday. However, while I was away, Julian Wellesley somehow got wind of our plans. On my return, my secretary called me at home to warn me that a meeting had been scheduled with him first thing on Monday morning.

At the meeting the atmosphere was initially reasonably cordial but, once I had confirmed my intention to resign, the conversation became less friendly. In an attempt to persuade me to stay I was offered, but I declined, the role of Chairman of two new ventures which, Julian suggested, might be set up in New York and Hong Kong. He then asked about my plans for the new company, Richard's role and how it was to be funded. I emphasised I had no intention of trying to persuade clients to leave with me – something about which I felt very strongly. By now, I think he felt less uneasy about the prospects of a breakaway group leaving with part of the business, but he reminded me that I had more than half of a five year contract to run and that I should not expect to be leaving any time soon. Richard was then asked to his office and he left CBC shortly thereafter. When I told Angus Maitland of my plan to leave, he decided to return to Scotland. I expressed the hope we might be able to work together again once our business became established and we agreed to keep in regular contact.

It was now the Spring of 1979 and we were briefed by the Association of British Insurers about what was to be the most important presentation CBC had yet undertaken. The ABI were concerned that the Labour Government had plans to nationalise the insurance industry and, after an initial vetting, we were asked to present campaign ideas to counteract the threat, in competition with a number of leading West End agencies including Saatchi and Saatchi.

We developed a campaign which we researched thoroughly and was shown to be potentially very effective in addressing the main issues. So, despite the calibre of the competition, we felt confident about winning the business. We were third to present on May 2, the day before the General Election.

On May 4, Margaret Thatcher, having won the previous day's Election, became Prime Minister. So there was no longer any need for our campaign. Never had CBC been more pleased not to win a new assignment!

I was now increasingly in a state of limbo, being less and less involved in planning and decision making. Meanwhile, as Richard had now left CBC, we agreed he should start looking for a suitable office of around 1,000 square feet in the area between the City and West End, where rents were a little cheaper. We produced a Business Plan which targeted a profit in the first year and secured some additional backing from members of Richard's family who took 15% of the company's equity. We both agreed to take a reduction in salary – in my case of 40%, Richard a little less. Through an introduction from my cousin Alan Butler, a lawyer at Simmons & Simmons, we appointed solicitors, whilst Arthur Young and Barclays were appointed accountants and bankers respectively.

I was now starting work on CBC's Budget for the coming year, which became somewhat difficult as there was no replacement Chief Executive with whom I could discuss its feasibility. I had always targeted a minimum of 20 % year on year growth and saw no reason to change this, but I did invite the CBC board to assess whether they thought this was feasible once

I had gone. In the end a compromise was agreed of around 10% – not especially demanding.

Richard, meanwhile, had seen a number of offices of varying suitability and we eventually agreed to take a lease on 1250 square feet at a rent of just over £10,000 p.a. on the top floor of a building in Southampton Row, which gave us a meeting room and six other offices. It needed to be decorated, carpeted and furnished, telephones had to be installed and other equipment purchased, but by early October it was ready for occupation and on Columbus Day it was open for business.

Back in Farringdon Street the atmosphere in CBC was reasonably civilised. I was continuing to attend monthly Group board meetings and now that Richard and I were separated I suspect my colleagues felt there was no danger of unethical behaviour – I intended to keep it that way.

It was now agreed that November would be my last Group Board meeting and that a farewell dinner would take place at the Mirabelle, after which I would leave.

The dinner was relaxed and despite some obvious unhappiness about my intentions, my colleagues were all magnanimous in wishing me well.

So, in December 1979, Richard and I were reunited in our new offices and, after sorting out a few minor last minute problems, we left for our Christmas break ready to face whatever challenges might lie ahead in the new decade.

Not As Planned

At that time, we had little idea how successful, eventful and ultimately challenging those years would prove to be.

6

Valin Pollen

The early days of any new company can be remarkably mundane and progress may, sometimes, appear to be glacial. It would be good to be able to report that we hit the ground running, but in practice, whatever the business, it's crucial to get the right systems in place, to be disciplined in using one's time, dedicate all one's energies to securing clients and be flexible and ready to tackle any project, however small. So at first and with help from our PAs, mine, Penny Rome, who had joined me from CBC and Sarah Emanuel who had just been recruited by Richard, we concentrated on the basics. We made a comprehensive list of everyone who we thought might give us business or be instrumental in introducing it to us, and we sent each of them a letter with a small brochure to let them know we were operational.

We were particularly gratified to get a good response from our media contacts and we ran a slightly cheeky advertisement in the FT in the form of a memo, aimed at the agencies, other than CBC, with whom we expected to be competing. In it we announced our arrival, told them they now had serious competition and warned that without a rapid change in their approach to financial and corporate advertising, Saatchi could soon be moving into the City. Not earth shattering but certainly tree shaking and it gave the market a clear picture of our intentions.

Our objective was to provide senior management of companies and financial institutions with a flexible resource that would be relevant to any communications brief. We believed our knowledge and experience would enable us to provide objective advice on a range of communications techniques, enabling us to plan, pre-research, devise, manage and monitor the effectiveness of our work on their behalf.

But the priority was to win clients. Richard had already completed a couple of small projects and we were also working for Guinness Mahon, the Merchant Bank. Meanwhile, I had been invited to a Reception at the House of Commons where I met Keith Young, an interesting and multi talented entrepreneur, amongst whose many interests was the House Magazine. We talked briefly about the magazine's importance as a medium for communicating with MPs, Civil Servants and other opinion formers and I pointed out that it should be better promoted as a medium for campaigns similar to 'Patients before Politics' with which I had been involved at CBC. He agreed and shortly afterwards

VALIN POLLEN

Premier House, 150 Southampton Row
London WC1B 5AL
Telephone 01-278 2933

To: Dewe Rogerson   From: VALIN POLLEN

     Extel Advertising

     Foster Turner & Benson

     St James's

     Streets

     Walter Judd   Date: January 1980.

We thought that you, and possibly one or two other readers
of the Financial Times, might be interested to know that
we are now fully operational at the above address.

We believe that the experience we gained in helping
Charles Barker City to become Britain's largest company
specialising in corporate communications will prove to
be invaluable in assisting companies, banks and other
institutions to tackle the increasingly complex, yet
vital communications problems of the 1980's.

We are quite certain that, being long established and
successful companies, you are also ready to accept this
challenge and that you have the dedication and range of
public relations, advertising and design skills to provide
a highly personalised, imaginative and cost effective
solution to your clients' particular and varied needs.

However, a little competition can only help to improve
standards generally, so we hope you will welcome our
arrival as a positive development designed to contribute
to the overall pool of accumulated knowledge.

Because without new ideas, we may find Saatchi's in
Threadneedle Street before they get to Madison Avenue!

Our launch advertisement

became one of our first clients – he also kindly printed our first letter heading. I also met the head of communications at the English Tourist Board who responded positively when I mentioned my background in CBC and we agreed to meet again to discuss how we might support his work to raise ETB's profile.

Our mailing had started to pay dividends and soon RHP Bearings, The Kensington Close Hotel and ETB became clients. Meanwhile our work for Guinness Mahon was growing rapidly as we handled PR, advertising, design and research projects and also launched an investment fund for them.

By now, we had just made our first monthly profit and we realised that in order to accelerate growth we needed to reinforce our small team. Neil Hedges was recruited as an account executive and Leslie Clarke as our accountant. Not long after this we were joined by Chris North to take control of all print and press Production.

This was a timely hiring as we had just been appointed to handle a communications programme for the launch of Kenana Sugar which was to become the largest sugar estate in the world. Situated in The Sudan at the junction of the Blue and White Nile, our brief was to develop a campaign to announce its launch, which involved the creation of a corporate identity, corporate brochure, film, advertising, PR, an FT Supplement, press packs, invitations and place cards etc. This was a massive project for a small team and gave us excellent experience in handling a totally integrated communications campaign. It was both exhilarating and exhausting. Whilst in The Sudan, I found the experience of being exposed to 50 degree temperatures extremely uncomfortable – especially a two hour drive around the estate by Ron Colley, the project manager, in a Land Rover without air conditioning!

* * * *

It was nearly a year after Richard Pollen had left CBC that he had lunch with an old friend from Metal Box who had been one of his past clients. Seemingly Metal Box felt the standard of creative work had deteriorated at CBC and it was agreed we would take part in a competitive three way pitch for the business. We were successful and greatly appreciated this act of faith in awarding the business to such a small new company.

Shortly after this, we had the opportunity to make a presentation to Gulf International Bank. We were conscious of being much smaller than the competition, among whom was Dewe Rogerson. We heard they had suggested we did not have sufficient expertise to handle such an important assignment, so Richard and I decided that apart from giving a good presentation we would need to increase our apparent size. One or two 'extras' were brought in on the day to give the impression of scale and activity. Once again we won the business and our name was now beginning to appear in the columns of Campaign.

Our financial year ended in September and we were on target to make a small first year profit, as we had forecast in our Business Plan. We now felt sufficiently confident to recruit an Art Director, Reg Pauffley, and I called Angus Maitland to enquire whether he might be prepared to consider returning to London yet again. I couldn't have been more delighted when he agreed and he joined us towards the end of the year. Shortly after that, he made a successful presentation to Staveley Industries and our imminent prospects now began to look very much more secure.

We had refined our marketing strategy and were now offering potential clients either a 'supermarket' style of integrated communications service combining advice on strategy, research, PR advertising and design or, alternatively a ' boutique ' service focussing on one particular marketing resource. We believed strongly in research, both to refine the client's brief but also to shape our strategic thinking and the quality of our ideas. This important resource was initially headed up by Angus Maitland, whose meticulous analytical approach made a unique contribution to the content of many of our subsequent presentations.

Perhaps not surprisingly, we had now outgrown our office in Southampton Row and after a short search we took a lease on a 3,500 sq ft Georgian property in Bedford Row which provided more prestigious accommodation. We moved there in the Spring of 1981 and expected it would be adequate for the next couple of years as it had sufficient space to accommodate at least 30 people.

There was an increasingly pressing need for a Creative Director which led me to contact Chris Greening, who had headed up our creative team at CBC, but now operated as a freelance consultant. I enquired whether he would consider joining us and was delighted that we were able to agree a mutually acceptable arrangement. He now became yet another very important part of our fast growing company.

A few months after this, Maurice Saatchi asked me if I would like to join him one afternoon for tea. He had noticed the speed with which we were growing and wondered whether we might care to consider selling and becoming part of the Saatchi & Saatchi Group. I politely declined, pointing out that since starting we had barely had a moment to take the packaging off our furniture, although we were hoping to get fully operational quite soon!

We were starting to attract more financial services clients such as unit trust managers, life assurance companies and insurance product providers for which we required account directors who had specialised financial services expertise. Such individuals were not always easy to recruit and I now found I was spending a considerable amount of time interviewing potential candidates.

To underline the importance of research, Angus proposed that we establish a Research and Planning

Unit which, apart from helping clients to formulate strategy, would commission external research on topics such as the perceived effectiveness of communications and also how major companies' communications were rated by City audiences. These studies were published regularly in the FT or The Times and were also very helpful in continuing to raise our profile.

* * * *

That Autumn, we ended our second year, ahead of forecast, having achieved another very solid Profit despite the investment in larger premises and more new people. We now decided to target a doubling in size of both Income and Profit for the coming year. Such a strategy would require more clients, more people and more space and early in 1982 we were once again looking for larger offices. We located a handsome 8,500 sq ft building on the corner of Grosvenor Gardens and Ebury Street and took a 12 year lease at a rental of £110,000 for which Richard and I had to give personal guarantees. Quite an increase from the rent just over two years earlier.

At around this time Richard, Angus and I felt we needed to think more carefully about the longer term direction of the company and its future objectives. I was also acutely aware that we did not have a particularly close relationship with our bankers and I began to question whether we had reached the stage when we needed a heavyweight Finance Director, should we contemplate making acquisitions at any stage in the future. I had kept in close and friendly touch with Michael Horstead, the Charles Barker Group's Finance Director, who had previously filled that role at the publicly quoted advertising agency S H Benson. We discussed whether he might consider joining us and we were fortunate when he agreed to become our Finance Director, working with us three days a week. I had huge respect for Michael, and his wise counsel and thoughtful advice was indispensable to me in the years that followed.

We now were given an opportunity to present for what was to be a game changing opportunity in our corporate development. Standard Chartered Bank put their international advertising account up for competitive pitches and we, together with Young & Rubicam, JWT and Saatchi & Saatchi, were shortlisted, We were very conscious that with no more than 40 people and no overseas offices we were heavily outgunned and possibly even outclassed, so we knew we had to produce something very special to stand a chance of winning. Angus Maitland proposed that we should undertake a research study among Finance Directors and CFOs in Tokyo, Frankfurt, New York and London, to assess their views about the effectiveness of current advertising by international banks, and the relevance of the messages they were communicating. Armed with this information, we asked three creative teams to respond to the brief and shortly afterwards they were ready with their alternative approaches, which were also extensively researched before presentation.

The presentation commenced with the findings of the research which, perhaps not entirely surprisingly, revealed that almost all international advertising by major British, American, Swiss, German and Japanese banks was considered to be irrelevant. Worse still, much was also considered a waste of money. We then showed our three campaigns and outlined how each specifically answered the clearly established needs of the Bank's target audience and how they would give Standard Chartered a distinctive positioning. When we had finished, Lord Barber, the bank's Chairman, who had previously been Chancellor of the Exchequer in Edward Heath's Government, turned to his colleagues and perhaps half jokingly said 'I don't know about you gentlemen, but I think these chaps may know almost as much about banking – and possibly even more – than we do.'

We felt that augured well and a few days later we received the news of our success. Richard Pollen organised a highly memorable champagne breakfast in The Goring Hotel just opposite our office at which all involved celebrated this dramatic win. Richard now needed an Account Director to help him develop the campaign so I approached Howard Lee who had been a PR executive in CBC but more recently had been part of the communications team at British Telecom. He responded with enthusiasm and proved very adept at looking after the requirements of both advertising or PR focused clients. He was to become an important part of our team.

A growing number of clients were now seeking our help with the design and writing of corporate brochures and Annual Reports, many of which often failed to reflect the style and success of the company for which they were intended to be an ambassador. We considered the Annual Report to be the most appropriate vehicle for delivering an authoritative message of business confidence and we attached a great deal of importance to our work in this area. The requirement for more eye catching design and artwork within these Reports now led us to create a new subsidiary, Falcon Designs, in order to accelerate our production capabilities.

* * * *

In early 1983, Michael Horstead and I had a far reaching discussion about the future for the company and our corporate objectives, Would we continue expanding via organic growth, should we consider making acquisitions, might we even consider selling the company – there had been other approaches since I had tea with Maurice Saatchi – or should we consider floating on the Stock Exchange . Michael offered to prepare a paper for the board's consideration in which he would evaluate the merits of the various options.

Michael's paper was unequivocal. In view of our rapid growth to date and our ambitious expansion plans, he proposed that we should start planning immediately for our shares to be quoted on the USM. He recommended this course of action for four reasons – it would enable us, when required, to raise money, it would heighten our profile in the City, it would help us to be able to offer shares rather than cash when making acquisitions and it would mean we could introduce a share option scheme to reward key members of management. He did, however, point out that it would mean a great deal of extra work which might prove disruptive. After a fairly short discussion, Richard Pollen and Angus Maitland agreed with me that this was the right course of action for us and that Michael and I should proceed accordingly.

As a first step we needed to appoint brokers. Richard had a friend at Capel Cure Myers, Angus had contacts at Hoare Govett and I had dealt previously with James Capel. Beauty parades were sought from all three and we had the pleasure of being on the other side of the table as they pitched to us. Initially we felt Hoare Govett had been marginally more impressive but the relentless expression of enthusiasm from the main point of contact at James Capel finally led us to appoint them.

The opportunity to acquire more banking clients now arose with requests for presentations from Westpac – which had recently been formed as a result of a merger between BNSW and Commercial Bank of Australia to create the largest bank in Australia – and also National Bank of Kuwait. The latter involved a presentation to the board in Kuwait City and Stephen Anson, the designated Account Director and I found ourselves in Kuwait at a time when many Kuwaitis chose to be elsewhere, as a result of temperatures in the upper 40s. Fortunately on this occasion there was abundant air conditioning and we also won the business.

With our Research and Planning Unit growing so rapidly, Angus proposed that we should establish it as a separate company and profit centre. We recruited David Burton from the highly respected research company, Taylor Nelson, to head up the new company – Consensus Research – which absorbed the RPU and thus became our second self grown subsidiary.

And now for a light diversion. The insurance company, London Life, was a client with which Angus Maitland and I had been involved since we won it a couple of years earlier. We were now both invited to attend the company's senior management dinner in Bristol. Unfortunately, Angus was scheduled to make the first of a number of important new business presentations in the City first thing the following morning. We checked on the feasibility of catching a train leaving Bristol for London at around midnight, found it was impractical and decided to hire a car on arrival in Bristol and leave it at the hotel in order to drive back to London once the dinner was over. As usual, whenever Angus and I were going anywhere, one or other of us seemed to be tied up until the very last minute. However, we got to Paddington with a couple of minutes to spare. By the time we arrived in Bristol it was dark and we went straight to pick up the hire car. When we arrived at the hotel we gave the car keys to Reception so they could park it and told them we would be leaving much later in the evening. As we weren't staying, we didn't bother to take a room and quickly changed into evening dress in one of the cloakrooms, left our bags with the Concierge and then went to meet our host. A pleasant evening with two or three speeches ensued – one of which rather gratifyingly complimented us on the work we were doing for the company – and at around 11.15 we took our leave, explaining we had to drive back to London.

We went to Reception to pick up the car keys but, as we hadn't taken a room, they weren't there. We were directed to the Night Manager who asked us for the Registration Number of the car which, being a hire car, neither Angus nor I knew, He then asked if we could tell him the make and colour. Again neither of us could be certain of this as it had been dark and we had been in a great hurry when we collected it. We were then shown a rack with what appeared to be hundreds of car keys. Now, with growing concern I searched through them to see if I could recognise the right key. Fortunately, I found one with the car hire company logo on the fob. We then enquired where we might find the car and were told it had been put in a public

Car Park some distance away. This did not augur well for the fast return to London. We walked off quickly in the direction we thought was correct but in the absence of anyone from whom to ask directions – it was now nearly midnight – we realised we had little hope of finding it and we returned to the hotel. The Night Manager, realising we were now fairly stressed, organised the hotel minibus to drop us at an open air Car Park where we now started, in the darkness, to try to find a car to which our key would fit the lock. Finally, we found the car, jumped in, I started the engine, put it in reverse, took off the handbrake and accelerated – nothing happened so I pushed my foot harder on the accelerator – we were still not moving. Angus jumped out to see if there was an obstruction behind one of the wheels. He found the back wheels were spinning and digging in to soft sand and hence making no purchase.

We searched for something to put under the wheels, finally managed to get the car out of its space and drove around to find the way out. In the darkness we located an unmanned barrier at the Exit but without a ticket or anything else that would release it we were at a loss about how we would be able get out. I decided there was no other option but to try to lift it manually, but after a great deal of heaving, shaking, pushing and pulling, the barrier came away in our hands and fell to the ground! By now it was nearly 12.30 and a combination of relief coupled with exhaustion and frustration gave way to wave upon wave of hysterical laughter as we drove around the unfamiliar Bristol One Way system trying to find the exit to London. We finally calmed down and located the correct road to take us to the motorway. As many know, I tend to be quite a fast driver, but never was the journey back to London accomplished so quickly. We arrived back in Grosvenor Gardens just after 2 am. Later that day Angus was successful in winning yet more clients.

Meanwhile, further senior appointments took place, with Andrew Boys becoming Client Services Director and Alan Bayley joining us from CBC.

1. CBC and Charles Barker Group
   Boards - a Seminar at the
   Compleat Angler.

2. A parting gift from
   Charles Barker City.

1. Richard Pollen - went on to create, and subsequently sell, Richard Pollen & Company. Now advises a small portfolio of private clients and consultancies. Also chairman of an insurance fintech enterprise.

2. Angus Maitland - founder of Maitland, Chairman of the AMO Partnership and formerly Chairman and Chief Executive of The VPI Group.

3. Micheal Horstead - formerly Finance Director of The VPI Group.

4. Jean Wadlow (Mrs Redman-Brown) - formerly Managing Director, Wadlow Grosvenor. One of the first three lady members of the Reform Club.

5. Before it all went wrong. TCO's office
   in Park Avenue - Don Carter, Angus
   Maitland and Reg Valin.

6. Brian Winterflood - Life President
   of Winterflood Securities.

7. Richard Thoburn - CEO of Thoburns/
   Greentarget and founder of Burnie's
   Foundation.

21 January 1983 campaign

Valin Pollen this week launches its first campaign for Standard Chartered Bank.

1 June 1984

Valin Pollen has been appointed by the Government to handle press and PR for the privatisation of British Airways.

EVENING STANDARD - 6TH DECEMBER, 1988

A busy £14m from Reg Valin's bigger family

Reg Valin: he won't b...

by Joanne Hart

VPI (the old Valin Pollen) forecast full year profits of at least £13.5 million in September.

So today's news that the communications group has made £14.1 million in the 12 months to the end of September hardly surprised the City and the shares remained at 129p.

Turnover has increased by 83% to £66.4 million and earnings per share climb 130% to 18.3p. The dividend is generous, with a final of 2.4p making a total for the year of 3.5p, up 211% over 1987, in response to institutional grumblings.

Profits have gone up by 340%, reflecting a major contribution from US investor relations giant, The Carter Organisation. VPI chairman, Reg Valin, would not say exactly how major, but Don Carter himself has notched up at least his maximum earn-out target—£19 million.

Under a new arrangement with Carter, agreed earlier in the year, this will trigger a payment of £25 million this coming January.

Some analysts are concerned about where all this money will come from, expecting VPI will incur large interest payments to finance it.

"Not so," says Valin. "Most of the money will come from cash flow and we will borrow only about $5 million."

VPI's dollar exposure has also fuelled City fears but the firm has hedged 85% of it at $1.65.

VPI says prospects for the year look encouraging with new accounts coming in over here and corporate activity in the US providing business there.

THE EVENING STANDARD: 30TH MAY 1989

Valin nibbles at troubled Barker

by Joanne Hart

VPI Group, the old Valin Pollen, has built up a small stake in Charles Barker, the troubled public relations and executive recruitment concern.

The stake is understood to be less than 5% but has prompted immediate speculation that VPI could be interested in all, or at least part, of Charles Barker.

Certainly VPI chief Reg Valin knows his potential victim well. He worked there for 20 years, rising to chief executive of Charles Barker City before setting up VPI with Richard Pollen 10 years ago.

Today he says: "We are watching events with keen interest."

Sources close to Valin suggest that he would like to buy Barker's PR division leaving the executive recruitment arm to Barker chairman, David Norman. Martin Sorrell of WPP tried to do this last year but allegedly fell out with Norman over the pricing of a deal.

Since that time Barker shares have fallen by nearly 50%—although still on a higher multiple than VPI—and only this month Norman warned that interim results would not match up to last year's figures.

29 April 1983 campaign

The Wall Street Journal Europe, which is published by Dow Jones, has appointed Valin Pollen to be responsible for promotion and business advertising.

WALL STREET JOURNAL (EUROPE): 22ND FEBRUARY, 1989

VPI Group Will Seek to Establish Presence In Japan, Continuing Its Expansion Drive

By JOANNA NEWMAN
AP-Dow Jones News Service

LONDON – VPI Group PLC, after more than tripling pretax profit last year with a major U.S. takeover, said it plans to keep up the momentum with an assault on the Japanese market.

Talks last year to take over an unnamed Tokyo consultancy fell through. But VPI officials now say the British investor-relations consultancy and financial-advertising concern is considering taking stakes in and forming joint ventures with Japanese...

Pilisbury Co., in its fight against Grand Metropolitan PLC; and Batus Inc.. in its battle for Farmers Group Inc.

Yet despite VPI's overseas expansion British investors continue to undervalue the company because they overemphasize VPI's reliance on the vulnerable U.K. financial sector, said Lorna Tilbian, an analyst with Warburg Securities Ltd.

Vulnerability Is Exaggerated

But the worries about VPI's vulnerability to London's financial markets may be...

minority stake in a Japanese company and build it up or form a joint venture," said Mr. Valin.

"It's very difficult to establish good will in the highly protective Japanese business world unless it's through a joint venture," warns Christopher Akers, analyst at Citicorp Scrimgeour Vickers. A possible partner could be a securities house or bank with a ready-made list of corporate clients such as Nomura or Daiichi Securities Co., Mr. Akers suggested.

Valin Pollen International is expected to show interim pre-tax profits up to 31 March this year of £6.25 million, against the £1.2 million for the same period last year, when the results are released early next week.

CITY NEWS

The VPI Group Plc. Registered Office: 32 Grosvenor Gardens, London SW1W 0DH. Registered in England No. 1591284

CAMPAIGN: 4TH AUGUST 1989

Valin exit puts spotlight on Carter

by Emily Bell

The sudden departure of Reg Valin from the executive chairmanship of the VPI Group he has headed for the past ten years has surprised the City and reawakened speculation over the future direction of a group which has not enjoyed the best of times recently.

From the end of October the more dour, and some would say hard-nosed, Angus Maitland will take control of the group. Top of his list of priorities will be sorting out problematic US subsidiary The Carter Organisation, which has suffered falling profits.

VPI paid $114 million for The Carter Organisation in 1987 and is still paying Carter instalments on an earn-out system. The move was billed as Valin's, though Maitland was also keen to add to the group's investor relations capabilities, and it radically altered the balance of the VPI Group.

Of the total group profits, 60 per cent is provided by the Carter business, which is why the group's profit forecasts have taken a dive in 1989.

Merger and acquisition activity has dried up in the US market leaving Carter with drastically reduced revenue.

Valin . . . his departure has fuelled speculation over future of VPI Group

Forecasts for the full year to September now stand at £11 million, compared with the £14 million pre-tax profits last year.

Speculation about Carter's future has been rife since last Friday when Valin announced he would be stepping down into the role of non-executive deputy chairman, but the VPI Group line is that there are no plans to alter the relationship.

One possible scenario would be the sale of The Carter Organisation back to the flamboyant Don Carter

himself which, if it raised the right price, could extricate the group from its current problems.

Maitland will only admit that the US giant is not performing well. "We will be working hard to reverse that decline but there will be no shake-ups," he said, describing Carter as "a good effective colleague".

It is clear, however, that Maitland will not be prepared to wait for market conditions in the US to improve before trying to bring Carter's profits up to scratch.

Carter himself, the key to the business, was keeping a low profile this week and was not available for comment.

Maitland maintained that if Carter was looking for a management buyout "he would have shared that thought with us".

The inability of the otherwise healthy group to withstand the problems which Carter has thrown up may well be behind Valin's decision to step down.

The share price is currently at 109p after hitting a low of 107p

when the news broke last Friday, and the depressed price could have fuelled internal pressure for Valin to take a less prominent role.

"I'm not conscious that it is a bad time to go," said Valin, who stressed his decision was made entirely on the basis of it being necessary to find a younger successor so that he could have more time to himself.

But at 51, by chairman standards Valin is hardly an old man, and this has added to the speculation that there is perhaps a further reason for his choosing now to go.

Maitland is certainly likely to cut a harder-edged figure. He joined the group six months after it started in 1980 and has been working as Valin's right-hand man for the past few years.

As well as board responsibilities, he has used this expertise in investor relations to set up Carter Valin Pollen.

Valin has himself had a high profile in the industry, and he says Maitland will continue that. "It is a deliberate policy to have one person as the mouthpiece of the organisation," he says.

But it will be no easy task for Maitland to take over the reins of a business which is still uniquely identified with its founder.

Richard Koch - Management Week, June 1991

SO FAREWELL THEN, DEAR REG

Spare a thought now for Reg Valin, who founded and built up Valin Pollen, the most successful PR agency of the eighties until Reg bought the Carter Organisation, run by the eponymus Don Carter. That one move sank Valin Pollen. Reg's shares, once worth about £10 milion, became virtually worthless. Unlike many founders of quoted companies, Reg refused to sell his shares on the way down, even though he must have known the bad news ahead. Reg felt that to do so would be disloyal and send the wrong signal to his staff. He also

believed there would be a revival.

This month sees the integration of Valin Pollen into the American firm, Gavin Anderson Associates. The Valin Pollen name will disappear, and with it Reg Valin's claim to fame. This is a personal tragedy, because Reg was one of the most talented and genuinely decent victims of the late eighties' merger madness.

Does anyone out there have a new role for Reg, who remains one of the most creative men of his generation?

1. My daughter, Claire.

2. With Gitta in St. Paul de Vence.

3. Gitta and Madeleine Barretto -
   they share the same birthday.

4. Gitta in the South of France.

5. With John and Madeleine Barretto in Venice.

6. Keith Young - one of VP's first clients, founded the weekly House Magazine for Parliament; Sport First; Net Benefit and co-founded Easynet. Still at the helm, developing internet companies in the UK and overseas and now reviving Wight Fibre on the Isle of Wight.

7. With Bernard Anscomb in Nice.

8. David Gyle - Thompson - formerly Chairman of Whittards, Chairman of Onslow Boyd Venture Capital, on holiday in Austria.

1. With Peter Cruikshank in Vancouver.

2. Harriot Pleydell – Bouverie, founder and Chief Whisk, Mallow & Marsh.

3. Burnie, the inspiration behind Burnie's Foundation.

7

Valin Pollen International (1)

Work on our forthcoming USM flotation was now taking up a great deal of Michael Horstead's time and we had been asked to write the Introduction to the forthcoming Prospectus. I thought this would not be too great a challenge since it would largely reflect the activities of the company and our work for clients. Most of the rest of the document would be statutory information and supplied by our auditors. Little did I know about the Due Diligence process. After a draft of the document was passed to Simmons & Simmons for their comments, they responded with 120 questions, the first of which related to the opening line 'Valin Pollen was established in October 1979'. Their request was, please define 'established'!

There was a great deal more of this type of request for information including a requirement to see all senior staff service contracts as well as the contracts for every fee paying client – no wonder some companies approach this process with considerable trepidation, or even decide on reflection not to pursue it. We were proposing to have an all singing and dancing Prospectus contained in a glossy slip cover. Here we fell foul of the Stock Exchange Listing authorities who ultimately relented when we explained that over the years we had introduced many ground breaking creative ideas to enhance the effectiveness of communications and that this document was, for us, an immensely important promotional opportunity, embodying the essence of our company's creative skills and expertise. As a result we were able to score another first in the presentation of statutory information.

Once again we had outgrown our space and we were fortunate to find a building – 46/48 Grosvenor Gardens – with a floor area of 17,000 square feet – a few doors away from our present office. We now had a very difficult decision, whether to leave 36 Grosvenor Gardens and move to the other building, which would have doubled our space, or to keep 36 as well as the new building. Since we were again planning to double in size by 1985 we decided to take the risk and increase our space from 8,000 to 25,000 square feet and go all out for maximum growth which we hoped would be assisted by our Stock Market debut.

Meanwhile we were put through a Q and A session in readiness for the presentation James Capel had planned at the Institute of Chartered Accountants. Given the number of international clients for whom we acted and the proportion of income we generated from outside the UK, it had been decided to rename the Group VALIN POLLEN INTERNATIONAL. This became the holding company's name after we Listed on 31 January 1984. The presentation itself was attended by around 15 institutions, including an individual who sat high up in the lecture theatre and asked a number of very relevant questions. After the presentation he introduced himself as Brian Winterflood, 'Mr USM' and told us he made a market in all USM quoted company shares. He had particularly liked what he'd heard and would be following our fortunes closely in future. Brian was to become a very good and close friend of the company in the years ahead. He retired in January 2017 after 60 years in the City!

The float was a success and, with a profit forecast of £425k, the 110p Listing price went to a 40% premium in first day dealings. We probably agreed too low a price but as Capel pointed out 'it's important to leave something for the market.'

* * * *

One Friday afternoon, on the day of our annual staff party, Angus received a phone call requesting him to attend a confidential meeting at 5 p.m. in the City. When he eventually joined us later in the evening, he briefly told me about the Government's plans to privatise British Telecommunications in what would be by far the largest exercise of its kind ever undertaken. He had been asked to produce a paper on the implications of this decision, for consideration by Civil Servants and advisers first thing on Monday morning. When I got in just after 7 a.m. on Monday, I found Angus's secretary had nearly finished typing a 20 page document he had dictated over the weekend. British Telecom was to be the first in the Government's privatisation programme and Angus would be leading a team advising the company about communications, whilst Dewe Rogerson would act for the Government. This was an immensely important and prestigious assignment and massively reinforced our City credentials. It was also to be a huge success for the Government who raised just under £4 billion later in the year.

Some months previously, my hardworking PA, Penny Rome, had taken on responsibility for our administration, including personnel records, lease contracts, insurance policies, BUPA/ medical checks etc. Her successor, Jo Neary, who had also been enormously supportive, now moved to work for Michael Horstead, whose workload had considerably increased following our float. I now needed to find a very capable replacement as soon as possible. I was fortunate to be able to recruit Jane Fernback, a highly professional and resourceful new PA. Her role was not only to work with me in my dealings with clients and on new business projects, but also to support me as Chairman and Chief Executive of a public company in my dealings with the financial press, analysts, institutions and private shareholders.

Valin Pollen International (1)

Our first major takeover battle now arose when one of Neil Hedges' clients, Booker McConnell was on the receiving end of an unwelcome offer from Dee Corporation. A hasty meeting was called by Booker's Chairman, Michael Caine, and Neil and I joined the other advisers led by Warburgs to discuss how to respond. Both the Chairman and Warburgs were emphatic that the bid should be fought vigorously on a number of grounds and they were confident that it would probably be referred to the Monopolies Commission. After some sabre rattling, press skirmishes and lobbying, the bid was, as hoped, referred to the Commission for them to deliberate on its merits. Meanwhile our work for Booker also involved us with the highly prestigious Booker Prize for Literature which in 1984 was awarded to Anita Brookner for Hotel du Lac – for once not a particularly controversial decision.

For some years I had known Tony Good of Good Relations, another Stock Market Quoted PR company, and held him in considerable respect. We had occasionally talked of bringing our two companies together in a merger which would have created a very broadly based business, since Good Relations were particularly strong in areas such as consumer PR and lobbying in which we did not have expertise. One afternoon at the RAC Club he and I discussed and agreed the possible basis for a deal. However, in the end it did not come to fruition largely because it would have been necessary to reduce the size of his very large

Group board, some of whom apparently did not care much for my personal leadership style or our rather competitive approach to business. On reflection, I have often felt I should have tried harder to deal with the potential obstacles, as I think it might have been a very interesting alignment.

Another major business opportunity now arose when Reuters initiated planning to become the first British company to simultaneously List its shares in London and New York. When we were approached it was clear we needed a US partner as we were competing with the two largest PR companies in the world – Hill & Knowlton and Burson Marsteller. I contacted Gavin Anderson, who had previously been a director of Hill & Knowlton and whom I'd known since I was MD of CBC. Gavin now ran his own financial communications company in New York and I enquired whether he would join our team. Not surprisingly he enthusiastically agreed and together we worked on the proposals. A week later, Gavin came over to London to join us for the presentation to the Reuters' board. When it was finished, Reuters' Chief Executive asked me whether, if they chose to appoint either H&K or BM in New York, I would be happy to work with either of them rather than Gavin Anderson Associates. Not an easy call. Sitting next to Gavin, I outlined how we had worked together on various projects over many years and why we considered him to be ideally suited to ensure the New York Listing was a great success.

However, I emphasised that it was, of course, Reuters' prerogative to choose whichever combination of capabilities they thought would be best suited for such an important Listing. After the presentation was over I apologised to Gavin, who agreed I had no option but to respond as I did, but Howard Lee, who was part of the presentation team, later said he felt Gavin had been quite hurt. We were appointed in preference to BM in London, although it was decided they would handle PR and IR in New York.

Reuters' Listing was a great success and a couple of weeks later I was asked to go to Zurich to talk to their senior management about the implications and responsibilities of being a public company and the rules with which they should familiarise themselves from the 'Yellow Book.' It helped that I had quite recently been through the same process myself. Interestingly I don't recall any other company seeking such advice – perhaps it was normally offered by their broker or investment bank.

* * * *

Since meeting Anthony Wreford more than five years earlier, I had kept in regular touch. In the meantime he had teamed up with Michael McAvoy a leading figure in the IPR, to create a corporate communications consultancy, McAvoy Wreford, whose offices were just a few yards away in Beeston Place. I was keen to persuade them to become part of VPI because we were frequently being asked to take on new clients in sectors where we already acted for one or other of those clients' competitors. After two or three constructive conversations, they agreed to an offer based on a multiple of their Turnover and, in October, moved into 36 Grosvenor Gardens which now had spare space as a result of VPL's move to 46/48 GG. Alan Bayley, who had joined us some months earlier in VPL, became Managing Director of the new company. This was now renamed McAvoy Wreford Bayley, Alan's appointment now leaving Michael and Anthony free to concentrate on clients.

Consensus Research was continuing to grow very quickly and, with an increasing number of clients from outside the Group, we felt it was important for it to be seen to be a fully independent company. Fortuitously we heard that 50 Grosvenor Gardens would shortly be coming on to the market and we were able to sign a lease and relocate them there early in 1985.

Our first Annual Report as a public company was published in 1985. It reported a doubling in our profit and highlighted six key objectives which I considered to be fundamental to our future – to work for major UK and international corporations and financial institutions; to develop a management structure able to meet the demands of a fast growing business; to ensure our capabilities were constantly being improved; to recruit and motivate employees of the highest calibre and to help them build stakes in the business; to develop a network of corporate communications

VALIN POLLEN
INTERNATIONAL PLC

Reporting good results is just part of our business.

Five years ago, VALIN POLLEN was established to provide clients with a unique communications consultancy service.

The service was to include corporate and financial public relations and advertising, research, investor relations, marketing consultancy and corporate identity design.

Five years on, we have a client list that includes some of the bluest of blue-chip names in international business — including three of the five largest companies in the UK.

And, in our first Annual Report as a public company, we recently reported turnover and profits for 1983/4 that were (again) more than double the previous year's.

To maintain growth, we're investing in the creation of new services for clients — as well as actively seeking to recruit senior and middleweight executives able to meet our (and our clients') exacting standards.

If you'd like to learn more about how we can help your business, please contact Richard Pollen, our Managing Director; and if you have relevant experience as an advertising or PR executive and would like to be considered for a post with one of London's fastest-growing agencies, please send him your c.v. in strict confidence.

In either case, we'll be in touch immediately.

VALIN POLLEN INTERNATIONAL PLC
46 Grosvenor Gardens, London SW1W 0EB
01-730 3456

Announcing our first results as a Public Company

companies in the world's business capitals and to achieve year on year growth in profit substantially in excess of industry averages. We also featured a chart from Marketing Week which showed us as leading seven other publicly quoted advertising and PR companies in having the highest number of growth elements in our services mix.

Subsequent analyst and press briefings led to some very positive headlines which were useful in attracting more potential employees and also possible acquisition prospects. It was one of these that now took me to Holland.

Thomas & Kleyn were a Hague based consultancy, much of whose work was similar to our own. Both Tom Martojo and Dolf le Conge Kleyn had previously invited me to visit them to find out more about their operations – now seemed an ideal moment to accept. I spent the day meeting their people and learning more about the projects they were handling. Over dinner they expressed admiration for our business model and said they would like to join the VPI Group. Back in London, we discussed a proposed deal based on a three year earn out which we were quickly able to agree with them. Richard Pollen and I then went over to The Hague to welcome them as new members of the Group. We hoped it would be the first link in a planned international network.

Not long after this, we concluded another acquisition, when APT Photoset, with whom we had enjoyed a long and friendly business relationship, also accepted an offer from us. APT had an excellent reputation within the industry for work of the highest quality and had an extensive list of advertising and design agency clients. They were to become a significant contributor to Group profits.

In the City there had been a great deal of talk about deregulation, known as 'Big Bang.' Massive changes in the way the LSE traded were planned, with a move away from floor to electronic trading and the way open for banks and larger firms to acquire smaller ones. London's turnover was currently no more than 25% of New York's, so there was a massive incentive to make the planned changes a success. We won this immensely prestigious assignment and were then asked to prepare proposals for a campaign with two principal audiences. The first, directed at an external audience to explain the reasons for the new measures and how everyone would benefit – the other audience, smaller firms and provincial brokers who appeared to mistrust the Stock Exchange's objectives. We presented to the Council of the Stock Exchange, chaired by Sir Nicholas Goodison, in what proved to be, at times, a somewhat moveable feast as members came in and left and others arrived as the presentation progressed. In the event, our proposals, which were enshrined in a series of more than four inch high documents, were approved and we were asked to implement the proposed programme which helped to pave the way in October 1986 for a revolution in trading practices.

No sooner had we finished that presentation than Howard Lee and I were on our way to Hill Samuel where, an hour later, we put forward proposals for one of the Government's next privatisations – British Airways. On this occasion, we were appointed to act for the Government rather than the company, with Saatchi working for the airline. I particularly recall that at the end of the first of many subsequent progress review meetings, the Transport Secretary, Michael Spicer, enquired whether there were any more questions. A voice piped up from behind those sitting around the table. ' I'm from the Treasury, how much is all this expenditure going to reduce the final proceeds ?' There was a man who had a very clear idea of his priorities! The company's successful market debut took place in February 1987.

Shortly after this, we had further success with our appointment as members of the Government's advisory teams handling both the British Airports Authority and Rolls- Royce Privatisations – in cooperation with MWB – as well as the flotation of the Wellcome Foundation. Meanwhile, MWB were appointed to handle the IPO of TV-am. These were all very challenging but highly stimulating assignments and, as always, continued to help us to maintain a high profile in our marketplace.

The privatisation programme had been putting particularly heavy pressure on Angus Maitland, for whom we had been seeking heavyweight reinforcement for some considerable time. After a lengthy search, we were able to persuade Dale Fishburn to join us as Director of Research and Planning. Dale, a Harvard graduate, had previously held a similar position at JWT and it was gratifying to be able to attract someone of such high calibre and quiet authority.

Richard Pollen now replaced me as Chief Executive of VPL and, after a lengthy search we appointed John Dembitz as Managing Director. John joined us from Charterhouse Japhet and his background as a McKinsey consultant was an additional advantage. Meanwhile Neil Hedges had been promoted to Assistant Managing Director earlier in the year to reinforce our senior management team.

Our rapid rate of expansion meant that we kept the head hunters extremely busy. In order to free Chris Greening for more creative work on behalf of the Group, we had been seeking a new Creative Director for VPL for quite some time. We were ultimately able to secure the services of Lucian Camp who had a fine reputation for his award winning creative work in a number of West End agencies.

I now found myself having to say farewell to my hardworking and immensely capable PA, Jane Fernback, who had become pregnant. Jane had joined just after our Stock Market debut and had taken on the additional responsibilities with great dedication and calm efficiency – I was very sorry to lose her. After the usual lengthy search, I was able to recruit Melanie Hulbert who proved to be a worthy and efficient successor who sustained my energy every morning with a much appreciated chocolate bar.

We had always been very committed to helping charities and had been one of the first supporters of Business in the Community. Now a direct opportunity arose for us to make a more tangible contribution, when Esther Rantzen sought our help to launch Childline. We felt especially privileged to be involved with such a worthwhile charity which, over many years, has given support and comfort to so many abused and misused children.

A little later, Barnardo's, whose Patron was Princess Diana, asked VPL to create a new corporate identity and assist with the charity's re-launch. Princess Diana took a very active interest in the work and we were again delighted to have the chance to make a small contribution to the activities of such a worthy cause.

But now we had to press ahead with international development.

8

The Carter Organization (1)

I was beginning to receive increasingly frequent calls from James Capel, enquiring about our international expansion plans – particularly in New York. We had associate relationships in place in Europe, Tokyo and New York but were finding more clients were seeking our direct involvement with PR projects in the US. Earlier in the year we had also been responsible for helping to launch The Wall Street Journal in Europe and had a number of American clients including Anheuser – Busch, Goldman Sachs and Gould, so we felt comfortable at the prospect of acquiring either a strategic stake in, or the outright purchase of, a suitable partner.

Over the years since becoming Chief Executive of CBC, I had made a point of regularly visiting New York and had developed a number of good media contacts who I hoped could be of assistance. I had also worked on projects with Doremus and Charles Barker Ayer Financial which I thought might also be useful.

Early in 1987, I started to pay more frequent visits
to New York to explore the possibility of reaching an
agreement with one or other of our local associates.
Our closest link had been with Gavin Anderson, with
whom I had previously discussed becoming part of our
Group. However, as on previous occasions, Gavin felt
my approach was premature as he wanted to be much
larger by the time we did a deal, so he would ultimately
earn 'top dollar.' I also talked to the highly respected
shareholder communications and proxy solicitation
specialists Georgeson – again without success.

Shortly after this, it was suggested I should contact
Don Carter whose Carter Organization was New
York's leading, and by far the largest, proxy solicitation,
investor relations and corporate governance specialist.
I gathered that Carter also handled a little financial
advertising and PR, but this capability could be
substantially increased if a deal could be done. So,
reasonably well briefed, Michael Horstead and I flew to
New York to meet him.

Carter had a lavishly appointed office in a stylish
building at the top end of Park Avenue. High up around
a central atrium, the office had apparently been used
for some of the sequences in the film *Wall Street*. Its
décor was smart and functional but it was very clear
that a great deal of money had also been spent to give
it an air of conspicuous corporate success. Carter's own
office was palatial with a considerable amount of glass
and black leather and was dominated by a huge desk

behind which were screens providing instant market information from New York, London and Tokyo. It was easy to see why *Wall Street's* film makers had felt it was an ideal set. Instead of an executive washroom he had a vast gym which would have not looked out of place in a five star hotel!

We briefed him at length about our company, how fast we had grown in the last seven years, our clients, our people and our Stock Market Listing. He was particularly interested in our decision to go public and I wondered whether this was because it was also on his agenda. He then gave us a similar overview of his business and emphasised the pre-eminent position TCO played on the US takeover scene, working with both leading investment banks and corporate raiders. Apart from this high octane activity, he also undertook investor relations, stock surveillance and shareholder relations programmes. He confirmed that TCO had a small financial PR capability but he expressed a readiness to hire more specialists if that aspect of his work increased.

I told him we were keen to make an acquisition in New York but were in no hurry, lest he felt we might have unlimited resources. We also emphasised the considerable potential for two way traffic in business which we hoped might flow from such a union. Finally we sketched out the probable basis on which a deal could be done – by acquiring TCO with VPI shares. For a first meeting we got on well and we both agreed to give the matter further thought and to talk again. Before leaving he told us he owned 100% of the stock so the decision would not involve anyone else.

Back in London, Michael and I gave Richard Pollen and Angus Maitland a detailed summary of the main aspects of our discussions and the issues that had arisen. I also gave them my impressions of Don Carter himself – a fairly tough and potentially abrasive Runyonesque character who was very much larger than life. We agreed it was now crucial for Angus to meet Don and to evaluate TCO before proposing a possible basis for a deal. From then on things moved remarkably quickly and, after a couple of further meetings, Don and I agreed we would go ahead with the proposed tie up and the outlines of a deal were also finalised. We then briefed our advisers – Goldman Sachs acting for Carter and Robert Fleming for VPI.

The basis of the deal was fairly straightforward. An initial cash payment of $50m. followed by three further payments in VPI shares, totalling a maximum of $63m., subject to satisfactory year on year performance. Whilst the bankers and lawyers got the ball rolling Michael and I talked to James Capel about a $50m Placing of our shares to produce the cash element of the deal. Capel did not envisage this would be a problem as, with the benefit of two full months of TCO profit, we were already forecasting a Group profit in excess of £4m.

At around this time, Michael had decided to become a non executive director, but not before the deal was completed, so once again the head hunters were briefed. On this occasion they had to find a Finance Director with public company experience. Michael and I interviewed a number of potential candidates, finally offering the job to Norman Lindsay who had a baptism of fire in having to handle our side of discussions on financial matters with Robert Fleming in London and Goldman Sachs in the US.

Meanwhile the first of an interminable number of meetings was taking place at which Robert Fleming, Simmons & Simmons, Arthur Young and James Capel made individual contributions to our Placing document. At the same time, Angus and I started to plan the content of a presentation to the investors who we hoped would be backing the deal. In this we were assisted by Chris North, who had recently joined me in VPI and became my executive assistant

We were increasingly optimistic about the likely response to the deal since we were convinced the City would welcome both its logic and considerable scope for synergy. Shortly after this, James Capel called me about the proposed Placing price. At that time our shares were trading at around 275p and, recognising that the deal was heavily earnings enhancing, they proposed that investors be invited to pay 400p – a 45% uplift on the current price. Bearing in mind our experience at the time of our float three years earlier, we argued for 450p and eventually reached a compromise at 425p – nearly 55% over the prevailing price.

When trading in VPI shares was suspended the price was 275p – after the deal was concluded on 31 July 1987 dealings recommenced at 550p – an extremely healthy 100% increase. Once everything had been finalised, Don Carter and his wife came to London to celebrate our new relationship and they joined the VPI board for a very enjoyable dinner to mark the tie up between the two largest investor relations and financial and corporate communications consultancies in their individual markets. The future looked to be full of promise.

Now we had to get down to business, starting with Don joining the VPI board in London and attending its monthly meetings. This was the era of Concorde and short visits could be made without too much interruption to busy schedules. Likewise, Angus Maitland and I now attended TCO board meetings at which Art Ross, TCO's President would also join us. At these meetings we reviewed the company's business development strategy, its financial performance and its new business plans and successes. It was immediately apparent its financial systems left much to be desired, so we approached Simon Strauss, who had been a senior member of the Arthur Young New York financial reporting team at the time of the deal, and appointed him to become the company's CFO.

As the year progressed, business opportunities continued to develop between the two companies and we asked Howard Lee to move temporarily to New

York in order to coordinate this activity. Emphasis was placed on improvements in systems, technology and operational management and international projects were undertaken for Goodyear, Monsanto and Xerox. Later in the year it was decided to create a new company in London, Carter Valin Pollen, with responsibility for VPL's UK investor relations clients. Its twin in New York became a new division within TCO. The company also took on additional space to accommodate its growing team of stock surveillance and proxy solicitation specialists. All seemed to be set fair for a highly productive and mutually beneficial relationship.

Not As Planned

9

Valin Pollen International (2)

At about 3.30 during the night of 15 October, I was awoken by an enormous crash behind my flat in Sheffield Terrace. The wind was howling and the rain lashing down, but in the darkness I was unable to see what had happened. As I discovered later, a huge plane tree had come crashing down in the communal garden – mercifully along its widest part, rather than on top of the surrounding houses. Downstairs, the double glass doors to a balcony were threatening to give way under the force of the storm and the noise was deafening. I was unable to sleep and decided to watch TV which was giving increasingly alarming bulletins about a massive storm in Southern England. At around 6.30 my PA, Melanie, called me. She had been up for hours and had decided to make her way to the office. She warned me that plane trees had apparently fallen all over London, particularly on the Embankment, and to be careful when driving in. For all Londoners this was an immensely stressful experience, but almost all our staff made it to work and at the end of the day we all breathed a sigh of relief. This was to prove premature and a lull before an even more dramatic storm.

On the following Monday morning, Stock Markets were in freefall all over the World, with losses on the main indices of well over 20%. Our share price was hit extremely hard, at one time being off nearly 35%, but it recovered slightly and settled at a loss of just under 30% by the end of the day. Perhaps unsurprisingly, a number of our shareholders called to seek reassurance that they should not sell in a plunging market. More tremors occurred during the week, but markets eventually stabilised and a gradual recovery started to take place. These events were, however, to have unforeseen implications.

Putting that behind us, it was nearly time for some year end celebration, VP Christmas parties, traditionally held in January, were invariably great fun and meticulously organised, with a great deal of attention being paid to ensuring that everyone had a thoroughly enjoyable evening. This was to be no exception – but first a little deception. Our parties tended to be held at The Savoy, but this year invitations were to the Strand Palace Hotel. Once everyone had arrived, I made a few remarks about how we had been hit by the crash and this was a year for a little belt tightening but, as the faces were clearly registering disappointment, I then said 'However, now isn't the time for it, so perhaps you'd all like to go across to The Savoy so we can get the show on the road.'

The Party had a circus theme and guests went down a Helter Skelter from an access door high above the room where we were to have dinner. On the floor, they were surrounded by jugglers, tightrope walkers, fire eaters, and clowns – creating the perfect ice breaker. After an excellent dinner the thespians among us put on an irreverent and highly amusing pantomime telling the story of Cinderella and her ugly sisters 'Val' and 'Polly' – customarily entertaining and particularly enjoyed by Don Carter, who was attending for the first time.

We now pressed ahead with a number of important management changes. Having completed his earn out, Anthony Wreford decided to leave MWB to pursue his personal interests. We wished him well since he had played an important role in building MWB and its excellent reputation. Dale Fishburn was appointed MWB's Chief Executive and was replaced by John Williams as VPL's head of Research and Planning.

At about the same time, Richard Pollen became Deputy Chairman of VPL whilst John Dembitz was appointed Chief Executive.

An opportunity now arose to put forward proposals for one of the largest PR accounts in Europe – Visa Europe, Middle East and Africa. Once again an enormously prestigious assignment which involved working closely with Visa's other international consultancies. Our recommendations were well received and we were delighted to be entrusted with such an interesting and high profile project.

Although a satisfied client is the paramount objective of any company in the service sector – as far as I can recall we only lost two or three throughout the years – it was always good to have independent recognition for the quality of our work. We were, therefore, particularly pleased to secure three awards for our Scottish client Low & Bonar – an IPR Award for excellence in investor relations, an ITVA award for a company video and also the Scottish Design Council's award for the best Annual Report in Scotland. Immensely gratifying and a spur to strive for even greater excellence.

* * * *

We had found that one of the most effective ways of developing relationships with potential clients, and to help win new business, was to lunch them in one of our meeting rooms, prior to which we would show a film about the company and its activities. These lunches were designed to create an informal environment in which we could have a relaxed discussion about a wide range of business issues, talk a little more about ourselves and gradually build a growing rapport with companies we hoped might one day become clients. Such 'in house' lunches were also very popular in the City and on one such occasion Angus Maitland and I were guests at an investment bank where we were asked to lunch at 12.45. On arrival we were told our host had regrettably been detained, but one of his colleagues proposed that we should start without him. By 1.45 we had virtually finished our main course when our host arrived, apologising for lateness as a result of appalling traffic problems. We had a friendly conversation over cheese and coffee and departed at 2.15. Afterwards Angus mentioned he had heard that the 'double lunch' was by no means entirely unusual in the City, with the host starting a first lunch just before 1 pm and then slipping away to join the second at around 1.45, having excused himself to deal with an 'urgent call.'

The breakfast meeting had now also become very popular as a means of squeezing yet more meetings into the day. I believe Angus holds the record by starting one breakfast at The Savoy at 7 am, moving on to a second just around the corner at The Howard at 8.15 and managing to get back to The Savoy again by 9.15. It's a mystery he still remains so slim – even if breakfast was merely coffee and orange juice and maybe one croissant.

MWB were continuing to expand, having been appointed to act for the Society of Motor Manufacturers and Traders in developing an educational programme for schools and pre and post Election briefings for MPs. They now hired Tony Iveson who had been working in PR for Granada TV. Tony had been a youthful Squadron Leader during the War and had flown both Spitfires and Bombers. At one time, a member of the Dam Busters, Tony had also been part of a squadron that attacked and sunk Germany's largest battleship, the Tirpitz. Tony was a highly decorated pilot and had an exemplary war record – an outstanding and truly courageous member of the 'Few'. VPI's year end results were well received in the City and our AGM was much better attended than usual, with more than a couple of dozen shareholders in the audience – including Peter Spencer – Smith and Kyrle Simond. Once we had completed the formal business, I invited shareholders to join the board for a more relaxed discussion over drinks. To my considerable surprise, Peter then rose to his feet and offered his congratulations on the results we had achieved, coupled with his hope that we would continue to double in size as we had done ever since 1984. A particularly touching moment, especially as I recalled our first meeting and the confidence he had placed in me at my interview around 25 years before!

Meanwhile there were yet more management changes. Norman Lindsay, VPI's Finance Director, had found it difficult to adapt following the TCO acquisition and was replaced by Peter Barfield, from VPL, as VPI's Finance Director. Don Carter became Chairman of VPI (North America) and Michael Horstead, who had so successfully steered us through our Stock Market flotation, now became a non executive director. At the same time, Richard Pollen, who had played such a crucial role in building VPL during its early years, also became a non executive director.

VPT&K had completed their earn out and the absence of Tom Martojo, now based in London, coupled with internal problems and client losses started to impact on their performance. This led us to conclude that Tom should return to The Hague as soon as possible. John Dembitz now replaced him as Group International Director and Neil Hedges was promoted to Chief Executive of VPL.

Whilst John Dembitz focused his attention on Switzerland, I had been trying for some time to persuade IR Japan in Tokyo to agree to a much closer relationship and a visit to Tokyo was accordingly planned in the early Summer. The night before leaving, I checked our company video, corporate brochures, annual reports, two language business cards etc. and set the alarm for 5.30 as I was scheduled to catch an early flight.

* * * *

At about 4.15 in the morning I awoke to find the room spinning. I lay still, but the spinning continued, so I worked my way with some difficulty to the bathroom and splashed my face with cold water. This appeared to be having no effect so I returned to bed hoping that whatever was causing the problem might gradually disappear if I closed my eyes. Unfortunately the spinning continued and by 5.30 I realised I would be unable to fly to Japan. Shortly after this I called my friend Dr Barretto who told me he would come over right away. When he arrived, he checked one or two responses and then, somewhat disconcertingly, told me he wanted me to go to hospital right away. He called the Wellington to book me in and having negotiated a tricky narrow flight of stairs to get down to my internal lift, he drove me straight to the hospital. Shortly after I had been admitted, one of John's colleagues, a neurologist, popped in to see me and after some more checks he uttered the disconcerting words ' we're not quite sure about the problem so we'd like to run a few tests.' I won't go into details, but whatever was in their armoury of options was tried, including a lumbar puncture to which Tom Martojo had been subjected a few months earlier as a result of back problems and had pronounced as being seriously unpleasant. Oddly enough I didn't find it too bad, but by then they'd experimented with so many other tests I think I was almost up for anything. Meanwhile the visit to Tokyo to talk to IR Japan was on hold.

The upshot of all the tests was that a couple of days later the room was still spinning, albeit less rapidly, and I was still feeling extremely unwell – possibly not helped by two days of being a guinea pig.

But very soon, worse was to follow.

Angus Maitland came to see me in the Wellington to enquire about my progress and then told me a problem had arisen with Don Carter. Apparently Don had called to say that in the wake of the previous year's Stock Market crash he was no longer prepared to take his scheduled first stage earn out payment in VPI shares. He was apparently most emphatic that he wished to receive his year end payment – $25m. – due on December 31, in cash. Angus and I agreed this was unacceptable but since I was feeling too unwell to discuss such important issues with Don, Angus agreed to talk to him. The next day he came back to tell me that Don had been extremely difficult and totally inflexible, having stated that he was already on target to achieve his 30th September year end forecast and if he did not receive cash he would not be coming in to the office and would take the rest of the Summer as a vacation.

In the face of such an unprincipled threat, there appeared to be no other option but to agree to his demands, so we contacted Barclays and Robert Fleming to secure the necessary loan. Perhaps not surprisingly, as we were forecasting a pre tax profit of nearly £14m. this was not a problem, but with base rate at 13% and thus the cost of borrowing at more than 16%, we would be paying over £2m. a year to service the debt, with loan repayments in addition. Not what had been planned at the time of the deal, and when it was put to them later in the year, far from popular with our shareholders.

A few days later I was discharged from hospital, still feeling somewhat fragile and with a diagnosis of a viral infection that had attacked an area of the brain which controlled balance – possibly caused by overwork. I decided to try to leave the office by 6 pm for a week or two, but inevitably that became increasingly difficult, particularly as the situation in Holland was continuing to cause concern.

Angus Maitland and I had been discussing ways in which international business opportunities could be developed through the cross referral of clients between Group companies. Accordingly, in the Autumn, we created a new operational board which Angus chaired and initially comprised Dale Fishburn, John Dembitz, Peter Barfield, Art Ross, TCO's President and Tom Hegedus who had recently joined us when his company HRH Marketing Research was acquired by Consensus. This now provided a real impetus for international growth.

VPT&K were still underperforming and Tom Martojo's return to The Hague had done little to improve the situation. After a review of the company's forward projections and an assessment of their morale, it became clear that the relationship was over and it was decided it would be in everyone's interests for them to become independent once again. We agreed an arrangement whereby they bought back 80% of the company, which would leave VPI with an ongoing minority interest and the chance for us to continue to work together to mutual benefit whenever the need arose. For me, this was a disappointing end to a relationship that had started so well and had been based both on shared values and a similar approach to our clients' communications challenges. It was, perhaps, a mistake to separate the founding partners, but when the decision was made it had appeared to be an opportunity to further strengthen our ties.

Both VPL and MWB continued to be approached to handle additional privatisation assignments and, at the year end, the future outlook appeared to be extremely encouraging.

* * * *

Christmas Day 1988 was on a Sunday which meant I had a four day break with plenty of time for reflection. I found myself thinking long and hard about the company's future and also my role as Chairman and Chief Executive. The health scare in the Summer had followed a number of annual medical checks during which I had been warned I had to slow down and that a 14 hour day and very few holidays were not conducive to good physical health, or well considered business decisions. I was very aware that all too often I felt like a Chinese plate juggler desperately trying to ensure nothing fell. There were also two other important personal problems, an elderly mother, in poor health and increasingly dependent upon me, and my daughter Claire who had been suffering for three years with mental health problems. Gitta and I were now separated and she had invariably taken sole responsibility for caring for Claire. I realised this could no longer continue as it was neither fair to her nor to Claire.

I finally concluded it was essential to plan a significant change in both my role and workload and resolved to set out the reasons for this in an explanatory note to Michael Horstead and Angus Maitland immediately on my return to the office. Michael and I then met and had a long talk about succession and the possible impact of such a change. However, I was now convinced, for personal reasons, this was a decision I had to make. We subsequently met Angus for tea at the Berkeley Hotel where I asked him if he would succeed me in October as Chairman and Chief Executive of the Group – on the 10th Anniversary of our launch. After a lengthy discussion about the responsibilities of the new role, he very generously agreed to my proposal and also that I should become Deputy Chairman. We also agreed nothing should be communicated until the Summer. Angus later reminded me that the occasion was somewhat enlivened by the presence of Koo Stark at an adjacent table!

Meanwhile it was to be business as usual and Angus and I continued to make regular visits to TCO to ensure they were taking steps to increase their investor relations and stock surveillance business.

We used to fly Concorde to and from New York in order to cut down on away time. On one occasion we had, as all too often, cut it a little fine to get to Heathrow, picking up a cab from Grosvenor Gardens less than couple of hours before the flight was scheduled to depart. When we told the driver our destination and deadline he told us we didn't have a chance as traffic was virtually in gridlock on Cromwell Rd. He was right, with less than an hour till take off we were still outside the V & A. As we crawled along, it was clear there was no chance of arriving in time if we stayed in the cab. We jumped out at Hammersmith and rushed into the tube where we grabbed tickets and ran down to the platform to see a train just departing. It was now half an hour before take off but another train arrived almost immediately and we reached Heathrow with just under 15 minutes to spare. We both shot off up a very long escalator two steps at a time and at the top Angus was already two or three yards ahead. He sprinted across the lengthy concourse to the Concorde check-in and I followed in his wake. At check-in, they called through to the plane which had already started running its engines. They then put us on a golf style buggy which dropped us at the Gate just four minutes before take off. Once seated, I turned to Angus and said 'That's once too often, we've got to stop cutting things so fine in future.' He then observed 'I didn't think you were going to make it when I saw you still half way across the hall – I've never seen anyone look quite so grey!'

Elsewhere, the Group's business continued to flourish. Consensus Research, which had earlier acquired HR&H Marketing Research International, had completed the integration of the two companies as HR&H Consensus Research and was actively winning business from inside and outside the Group. VPL had moved to new offices at 12/18 Grosvenor Gardens and continued to be involved in privatisation projects – for Seeboard, Manweb and Wessex Water whilst acting for the Government on the privatisation of Power Gen and

National Power. Meanwhile, Carter Valin Pollen worked with MWB on the highly visible launch campaign for Euro Disneyland.

And, as always, there had been yet more promotions including Dale Fishburn to the important role of Chief Executive (UK and Europe) whilst Andrew Boys became Managing Director of VPL and Ray Dafter, who had recently joined us from the FT became head of VPL PR.

When our half year results were announced in June, they were received for the first time with less than total enthusiasm. At just over £5m., six month profits were down nearly 20% over the corresponding period in the previous year. Whilst the UK companies were all continuing to perform well – up around 25% – TCO's high value merger and acquisition business had dropped by nearly 50%. The impact of the downturn was slightly softened by an increase in investor relations activity stemming from the relationship with VPI, but City commentators marked our share price down to show their disappointment. This was an extremely salutary experience which we intended not to repeat.

Shortly after this, at the end of July, the announcement was made of my intention to hand over the role of Chairman and Chief Executive to Angus Maitland. This would take place, as planned, in October on the 10th Anniversary of the founding of the company. I would become Deputy Chairman, Richard Pollen, my co founder, would be leaving the Group and

Dale Fishburn would join the Group Board. One paper greeted the news by commenting that Angus had an outstanding brain, an unflappable nature and brilliant long term vision, but was about to take on a Herculean task. In less than two months, and totally unexpectedly, it turned out to be a poisoned chalice.

Not As Planned

10

The Carter Organization (2)

A few weeks later, in early September, Don Carter
called. He claimed he couldn't speak on the phone as
he believed it might be tapped and that he was getting
the next Concorde flight to London to brief us about 'a
very sensitive issue'. He said he would be bringing his
lawyer with him!

We met the next morning with our lawyers,
Simmons & Simmons, also in attendance. Don told
us that the IRS had raided his office the previous day
and had removed a number of files and papers. Some
members of his staff had witnessed events and, not
surprisingly, had expressed concern about what had
occurred. When we asked him for an explanation, Don
was a little evasive but said that whilst undertaking the
expensive refurbishment of TCO's office in Park Avenue
he had asked the contractor to do some work on his
own apartment and that one or two of these costs
might have been charged to the company. There had
apparently also been a few examples of miscellaneous

expenses and other disbursements not being accurately recorded to specific client projects during Proxy battles and this had resulted in some rather arbitrary expense charging at the time of final billing.

After a fairly lengthy discussion about the possible scale of the problem and its implications, Don said he needed to get away in order to catch the Concorde flight back to New York as he was anxious not to be absent from the office in the event of any further developments. We were all understandably extremely shocked by this bombshell and, after he had left, we sought Simmons & Simmons' views about the implications of Don's highly disturbing revelations. Whilst equally concerned, they gave the impression that such events were not unheard of in the US, but that if what had occurred became known outside the company, the effects on TCO's reputation and its business could be very damaging. We subsequently spoke to both Robert Fleming and James Capel, both of whom expressed real concern about its likely longer term impact. They emphasised that there could be no more transactions in VPI shares, nor any further progress on deals which might involve issuing VPI shares by way of consideration. In the meantime, we took immediate steps to ensure that all expenses incurred on TCO client projects would be scrupulously checked in future.

Almost immediately after his return to New York, Don Carter called Angus Maitland to tell him that

The Wall Street Journal had heard about the raid on his office and wanted to talk to him about it. Angus advised him to say as little as possible and to avoid giving the journalist any information that might help him to develop a possible story. Don called back later to say he thought he might have quashed the speculation that had precipitated the call by saying he had been asked to provide some information to the New York State Authorities, but was unaware of the reasons for their request. The next day the paper carried an article claiming that Don Carter was being investigated for unspecified tax and other irregularities.

In London we issued a short statement confirming that the New York State Authorities had initiated an investigation in connection with which TCO, Don Carter and the Group were dealing with requests for information, but that at this stage we were unable to assess the extent of any potential liabilities.

Not surprisingly, many of TCO's clients were concerned to read about the investigation and despite efforts to deal with their questions, a gradual erosion of business began to take place. This not only had an effect on morale in New York but also led to a number of concerns being raised in London among both staff and shareholders – it also impacted on our share price. Our UK operations were in excellent shape but TCO's results were below expectations and when VPI year end results were announced in January, profits had shrunk to just under £6.5m. When these results were published, we also announced that Don Carter had resigned as Chief Executive of TCO but would continue as Chairman. The role of Chief Executive was to be shared by Art Ross, the company's President and Dennis Mensch, Executive Vice President and Director of Strategic consultancy. We hoped these appointments would reassure TCO clients that it was business as usual.

As the Authorities in New York pressed on with their investigation, VPI's lawyers in London and New York, and TCO's lawyers were kept extremely busy and increasing amounts of time and cost were being incurred. Six figure fees had already being incurred in the few weeks prior to the year end on 30 September. This ultimately led to the first of one or two not entirely friendly conversations with our bankers, who expressed concern about our ability to cover interest on their loans, the ever increasing legal costs and, of course, the repayment of what was to have been a fairly short term loan. We were able to reassure them that all was well in the UK and Angus Maitland, who had become Chairman and Chief Executive of VPI in October, outlined a number of cost cutting steps and increased marketing activities in TCO, all of which were designed to rebalance their business away from such a preponderance of Merger and Acquisition projects.

In order to strengthen our cash position the remaining 20% of VPT&K was sold to its management, providing a welcome injection to Group funds, but it signalled the end of a genuinely friendly and largely productive association.

In London, it was becoming increasingly apparent that morale among some members of VPL's senior management had been negatively affected both by media comment and contact with some of TCO's senior people. We hoped this was a passing reaction, but were well aware the problem could resurface if the situation in New York continued to deteriorate.

Angus Maitland, meanwhile, paid a number of visits to New York in order to discuss the ongoing legal situation with our New York lawyers Dewey Ballantine and the State Prosecutor. Neither assessment of the situation was particularly encouraging. Amongst other concerns, Dewey Ballantine mentioned that as well as Don Carter, the State Prosecutor was also pursuing Leona Helmsley, the so called 'Queen' of the Helmsley Hotel Group, for tax evasion. Her reputation in saying 'tax is for little people' was certainly not likely to be helpful to her – nor to Don Carter.

Back in London, Angus Maitland, Peter Barfield and I had an extremely uncomfortable meeting with Barclays who were now monitoring our monthly trading figures. They expressed considerable displeasure about the status of the security on their loan and also the ever increasing legal costs, particularly when placed against a background of falling profits. We were warned that unless there was a rapid improvement in the financial situation they would be taking steps to secure their borrowings. As a result, and under growing pressure from the banks to pay down their loans, arrangements were made for a programme of disposals. The first of these, MWB, was sold to the CGI Group – a sad end to a very productive relationship with a team of highly professional colleagues who had built a strong brand as an independent PR company under the VPI umbrella.

* * * *

Events were now beginning to move very fast in New York and Don Carter had been arraigned on charges of tax evasion and other irregularities. After lengthy legal interventions, he eventually pleaded guilty to grand larceny and personal tax evasion and shortly afterwards was sentenced to imprisonment.

We were now faced with even greater pressure from Barclays and Flemings. They pressed us to agree to an arrangement whereby a newly created company, TCF Partners, controlled by the Tranwood Group, headed by Richard Koch and Peter Earl, would acquire VPI and help in its recapitalisation and restructuring. Proposals for this Scheme of Arrangement were eventually put before shareholders at an EGM on 1st October and approved.

Additional pressure now arose when five senior VPL directors decided they no longer wished to stay with the company and tendered their resignations – they left to create a new company, Fishburn Hedges Boys Williams.

There was now a pressing priority to reinforce VPL staff morale which had been badly affected by this development so I arranged meetings with some of our major clients to reassure them about the stability of the business and also our ability to continue to deliver a first class service. Sadly, despite this, a number of them decided to make alternative arrangements rather than be faced with uncertainty.

In a further effort to reduce debt, HRH Consensus was sold to a company controlled by the original members of Consensus Research – but there was still pressure to raise yet more cash.

Now, Angus Maitland, exercising his right to terminate his contract following a change in control of VPI, finally left the company, having done everything he could to look after the shareholders' interests and help Richard Koch and Peter Earl to stabilise the situation. He initially became head of Burson Marsteller's global financial PR operations before founding the highly successful and greatly respected Maitland Consultancy. For me personally, a very sad end to a close and greatly valued professional relationship with such an impressive and immensely loyal business colleague. I am happy to say we have kept in close contact ever since.

By the end of the year, it was becoming clear that TCF had not provided sufficient working capital to meet the company's day to day cash needs, a problem that was exacerbated by a combination of reduced income from fewer clients and high fixed overheads. A new potential investor introduced by TCF Partners attended an emergency board meeting just before Christmas to discuss the possibility of making a £1m. cash injection if I would once again become Chairman. To this I readily agreed. However, after a five and a half hour meeting we were still unable to reach any agreement – as a result the future now looked extremely bleak.

* * * *

On the morning of 9th January 1991, the call came to tell us that it had been decided there was no alternative but to put the company into Administration and that a team from Price Waterhouse would move into our office the following day to take over the running of the business. I was asked to be as helpful as possible in facilitating their work.

Whilst so much had been happening elsewhere in the Group, Carter Valin Pollen headed by Howard Lee had remained relatively immune to contagion. It was now clear however, that it, too, would have to be sold. I had a couple of conversations with Gavin Anderson whose company, Gavin Anderson Associates, was now part of New York's Omnicom Group. We agreed Gavin would come to London with John Wren – who is now Omnicom's Chief Executive – to discuss the purchase of CVP by Omnicom and for it to become the London office of Gavin Anderson. The discussions went well and in mid January a deal was agreed. In order to strengthen the relationship, Gavin asked me to stay on for six months as a consultant and whilst in London he and I called on one or two of CVP's most important clients to enable me to introduce Gavin and reassure them it would be business as usual, with a further strengthening of the New York – London axis. The irony of this development did not escape me, in that four years earlier I had tried to persuade Gavin to become part of VPI. Had that deal taken place, our situation today would, of course, have been entirely different.

Over the next few weeks a further steady erosion of key VPL people and clients occurred and it was clear that Price Waterhouse had an absolutely overarching priority – to ensure that HMRC and the VAT Authorities' debts were discharged.

In the midst of this, my company car which had been given to me when I stood down as Chairman the previous year, was stolen. VPI had kept it insured under the company policy for the remainder of the year but now when it came to making a claim, with the company under Administration, the insurers' interest in the company, and my vehicle in particular, mysteriously evaporated.

There was now nothing more to do, other than take my leave of the Administrators, who no longer required any further assistance to complete their assignment. I left my black book of contacts, together with all my personal mementos in a filing cabinet in my office, as that seemed to me to be the most appropriate way to part company with everything I had sought to build, but now no longer existed

A new chapter in my life was about to begin which, for the first time, I approached with a slight degree of apprehension.

But for many of my ex colleagues it was perhaps all for the best, as they moved on to build even more glittering careers.

* * * *

On September 8, 1998, an article appeared in The Wall Street Journal stating that Don Carter's conviction had been overturned by a New York judge on the grounds that the prosecution had not informed him that their star witnesses had confessed to embezzlement when their testimony was used to pressurise him to plead guilty.

What extraordinary, unforeseen and far reaching consequences ultimately stemmed from such totally unrelated events. Surely one of the more dramatic examples of the Butterfly effect!

THE WALL STREET JOURNAL.

Donald Carter's 1990 Conviction Is Tossed Out by New York Judge

By Ann Davis Staff Reporter of The Wall Street Journal
Updated Sept. 8, 1998 1:06 a.m. ET

A New York state judge has thrown out the conviction of former Wall Street highflier Donald C. Carter, who as a proxy solicitor played a role in some of the biggest takeover battles of the 1980s.

Mr. Carter's career imploded after state prosecutors started investigating him for overbilling an all-star client roster of corporate raiders and charging certain of his personal expenses to his proxy solicitation firm, the Carter Organization. In March 1990, he pleaded guilty to grand larceny and to filing a fraudulent state tax return. Mr. Carter served 13 months in state prison and work-release programs out of a maximum four-year sentence.

Not As Planned

11

A Change In Direction

For what seemed like the first time in my life, I had the opportunity to consider my future. I thought a good starting point could be to take a holiday. I called my old friend in Vancouver, Peter Cruikshank, and told him I was thinking of paying him a long overdue visit and asked if he could recommend a hotel. A few days later, I was standing beside a window on the 17th floor of the Pan Pacific hotel, in a room with a panoramic view over the harbour and watching a seaplane fly across the bay and gently alight on the water less than 100 yards away – a wonderfully peaceful scene.

Over the next 10 days Peter and I, occasionally joined by his daughter Alex, visited just a few of the many interesting places in this beautiful part of Canada. A train trip through the Rockies was quietly awe inspiring, whilst a visit to the Empress hotel on Vancouver Island, which was clearly immensely popular with tourists, took one back to the style and slightly faded gentility of a long gone era.

Since his days in Charles Barker, Peter had become a property developer and he showed me one or two of the projects he had completed in West Vancouver. Spacious properties in idyllic locations with beautiful views looking down to the ocean and at prices less than half those of a comparably sized property in London. This gave me some ideas about what I might consider doing when I returned to the UK.

Once back in London and feeling suitably refreshed, I contacted a couple of estate agents with whom I'd had previous dealings and asked them to let me have details about apartments that had potential for refurbishment in Kensington, Knightsbridge or Holland Park. Almost immediately an opportunity arose in Sheffield Terrace and I appointed a builder, agreed a brief and work was soon under way. The project went reasonably smoothly, but I realised very quickly that it was crucial to employ an interior designer, rather than trying to source materials, bathrooms and kitchens myself. I was very fortunate to secure assistance from Nicky Hulbert, my ex PAs' sister and over the next few years we collaborated on a dozen or more renovations.

I needed funding to finance these purchases, so at the beginning of 1992 I decided to put my house in Addison Rd on the market. I had been warned I wouldn't get what I had paid for it in 1989, but I wasn't expecting over 100 viewings, some for the third time accompanied by colour boards and tile samples, before finally concluding a sale more than 18 months later.

A Change In Direction

I suspect I'm the only person to have lost 25% on the sale of his home. Never mind, I now had funds to press on with more projects. I was very fortunate to have an excellent solicitor, Bernard Anscomb, who subsequently became a good friend, to handle the conveyancing for me quickly and efficiently. On one occasion I exchanged Contracts on the purchase of a flat in Kensington and asked permission to start decoration in the five weeks before Completion. During that time new bathrooms and a kitchen were installed and it was completely redecorated, so by the time Completion took place all that remained to be done was re-carpeting and hanging curtains and blinds. I found a buyer 10 days later and it was sold within six weeks of the original purchase!

Later that year my mother died. Hers had been far from an easy life and I owed her a great deal, being a single child in a one parent family. She had been a strong influence in my early years and had always emphasised the values of integrity, fair play, care for those less fortunate than oneself and being determined to succeed in whatever one set out to undertake.

Over the years I have tried, unfortunately not always successfully, to adhere to those excellent lessons for life.

I was very keen to get involved with some form of charitable activity, as this had always been an important part of our work in VPL. I now became a trustee of McIntyre, which helped the disabled, and another very worthwhile charity – sadly no longer in existence – which had been created to help youngsters with entrepreneurial instincts to start small businesses. This was a great scheme, whereby school leavers were given funds to buy stock to sell in street markets and gradually build their marketing, purchasing and financial management skills. To my mind this is an idea that should be much more widely promoted as a way to help youngsters, without qualifications, to learn greater self sufficiency.

* * * *

At around this time I took out a subscription to Venture Capital Report, a magazine run by Lucius Cary and Dr Hamish Stevenson which gave Business Angels information about early stage or start up opportunities and the entrepreneurs who needed funds to develop them. I had one or two meetings with Lucius and Hamish at which we discussed the possibility of starting a Fund to invest selectively in some of the businesses featured in the magazine. Although Hamish appeared to be interested, Lucius already had an investment vehicle – Oxford Technology – so was disinclined to consider another venture. Some years later, in conjunction with Sir Richard Branson, Hamish was to launch the highly successful Fast Track series of league tables which are published in the Sunday Times and give details of the fastest growing small companies in the UK. This has not only focused attention on the contribution these companies make to the economy, but has also encouraged many small companies to aspire to be included – a great business initiative.

I now started to make small investments in some of the businesses featured in VCR. One of the first of these was a plan for the refurbishment of a block of flats in Liverpool, which was enjoying something of a renaissance following Michael Heseltine's high profile visit some years earlier. Unfortunately the promise of a makeover for the tired parts of the city did no reach the area of our development and the investment did not prove to be successful – I stuck to London from now on.

Now, completely out of the blue, I had a call from my friend John Barretto, one of whose patients was Princess Katherine of Yugoslavia. He told me the Princess had just parted company with Tim Bell and John had apparently suggested she should talk to me about her future PR requirements. I agreed to find out more about how I might help and to call her office to make an appointment. One morning a few days later, I met her in a small suite of offices in Park Lane which she and Crown Prince Alexander shared with a couple of assistants. She asked me how familiar I was with the overall situation in former Yugoslavia, politically and militarily, and we discussed both her and the Prince's objectives. Although she would have liked to play a more active part on the political front, as there were already so many other parties involved, I suggested that a more urgent priority was to provide humanitarian aid to those most in need. She agreed, and as she was scheduled to fly to the US that evening, she queried whether I could let her have a brief paper setting out one or two immediate priorities, for her to discuss with her husband before departing. As soon as the meeting finished, I dictated a short proposal to her PA and then left. She called me later and asked if I would be prepared to work with her to provide increased aid to the region and to raise the profile of her charity, Lifeline.

As a first step, I organised the design of a logo and corporate identity and also a free fundraising advertisement to run in a couple of Sunday papers. The next priority was a programme of dinners to raise further funds. Shortly after this, I was introduced to a highly efficient American woman, Tizzy Huttinger, who was Chairman of the charity in London. Various events were now planned in order to provide funding for essential aid projects. One of these was arranged at an exclusive Bond Street store whose owner was an active supporter of the charity. During the Reception it was announced that a raffle would be taking place with a number of luxurious items as prizes. One of the charity's volunteers came over to me and mentioned that ticket sales were not going too well and might I be able to help? I saw a couple of fur coated women standing alone sipping champagne and asked one of them if I could borrow her fur coat as a 'prop' whilst I sold raffle tickets. She kindly agreed and ticket sales soared. It is, of course, possible that one or two ticket purchasers might have thought the coat was one of the prizes – but everything was in a good cause. When I returned the coat to its owner a little later, her friend said 'Oh, thank goodness you're back, we thought you might have stolen the coat'. I assured her that it had been perfectly safe, but then its owner rather disarmingly said 'It wasn't so much the coat that was concerning me, it was the keys to the Aston parked outside which were in the pocket!'

It was now becoming increasingly apparent that Lifeline needed to be better organised and a great deal more professional in its operations. I approached my solicitor, Bernard Anscomb, to enquire whether he would be agreeable to reinforce the small management team and shortly afterwards he joined us to provide valuable advice across a wide range of important issues. Bernard is a great sportsman, having at one time been the World Over 55 Racquets Champion, he is also an enthusiastic Real Tennis and Lawn Tennis player. An active member of Queen's Club for many years, he was until recently a director of the Club and is now chairman of its Trustees.

Following one of our Lifeline meetings, Bernard and I met Lady Marks who was also actively involved in helping to get aid to those suffering in this tragic war. She was particularly concerned about the plight of those needing medicines and various pharmaceutical products and we discussed how I might help. Through my past relationship with Glaxo I was able to secure £1m. of medicinal products which had just passed their expiry date. With the help of a fleet of lorries provided by the Orthodox Church, once these containers arrived in Greece, we were able to transport them very quickly to where they were most needed.

* * * *

As a result of an article in Venture Capital Report I decided to make an investment in a new magazine for the games enthusiast – Games & Puzzles. Its editor, Paul Lamford, was something of a games polymath. Paul had competed in four chess Olympiads, on two occasions been British backgammon champion, had competed in the final of the poker World Series and won bridge cups in mini pairs championships including the Monte Carlo championship and the Tollemache Cup. A fellow investor was David Gyle – Thompson, Chairman of Whittards, the high street tea and coffee retailer. The magazine showed considerable promise in its early stages and attracted a solid initial readership but, during its second year, retail sales started to fall away and later in the year W H Smith decided to discontinue stocking it. Subscriptions alone were not sufficient to sustain the magazine and shortly afterwards it was decided to cease publication.

I had recently been asked by VPI's ex strategy director, Mike Potton, who was now a lecturer at the European Business School, whether I would be a panellist in assessing the Business Plans of final year MBA students. I was very pleased to do so as the

Plans were all very professional, highly imaginative
and impressively comprehensive. The students worked
in teams of four with roles covering the functions
of Managing Director, Finance Director, Production
Director and Marketing/Sales Director. Perhaps not
surprisingly they mostly featured fast food businesses
– possibly based on direct personal experience – but
they were well presented and persuasive and I even
expressed an interest in helping to fund the launch of
one of them. Unfortunately, all of the members of that
team came from different countries, to which they were
about to return after graduating.

The link with EBS and Games & Puzzles
subsequently presented a great fundraising opportunity
for Lifeline. With Mike Potton's help and Paul
Lamford's agreement we arranged for Paul to play chess
blindfolded against six of the EBS students in order
to raise additional funds for humanitarian aid. The
evening was a great success and, somewhat as expected,
Paul won all six games with considerable ease – an
extraordinary feat of memory.

Not deterred by the disappointing outcome to
our investment in Games & Puzzles, David Gyle –
Thompson and I decided to jointly invest in another
magazine, Prestige Properties. The magazine was
intended to be a rival to Country Life and, although
similar to the property magazines that were so
prevalent in marketing London properties at that
time, Prestige Properties was primarily designed to

be a shop window for quality properties situated outside the capital. It was well supported by estate agents' advertisements, but its distribution was mostly free, so profits were quite modest. After about three years, David and I concluded that it would never be a significant rival to Country Life, so we decided to sell our shares – thankfully at a small profit.

In 1994, Eurostar finally announced plans to inaugurate its passenger service to Paris in November and, remembering the press conference I had attended more than 30 years before, I applied for and obtained two tickets. On 14th November, Gitta and I joined a group of other passengers – most of whom turned out to be journalists – for this memorable trip. Whilst the journey across Southern England was fairly pedestrian, once in the Tunnel we all had an extraordinary sense of sharing a unique experience and applause erupted when we emerged on the other side. We now gathered speed and were soon travelling at about 175 mph, very much faster than I had previously experienced on a train journey in Europe, and reached Paris in around three and a half hours. Arriving in Paris, we were greeted by ranks of journalists and TV cameras all seeking interviews, a surreal but unforgettable experience.

David Gyle – Thompson and I often discussed his other business interests which were managed by his investment company, the Onslow Boyd Group, from a charming office and flat in Adam & Eve Mews. At that time, one of David's most significant investments was his ownership of Whittards. With help from his Managing Director, Will Hobhouse, who had held a similar position at Tie Rack, David had built Whittards up from a single shop in Chelsea to become a nationwide retail Group. He was now contemplating a float on AIM and we discussed VPI's experience at the time of our Stock Market debut and the changes in corporate life that would ensue as a public company. It seemed clear it would be a well supported Listing, so I made a point of applying for shares when the Offer took place some while later.

The merits of many other potentially attractive investment opportunities were occasionally discussed over breakfasts with Bernard Anscomb and two other friends, Dick Towner and John Heap – sadly these deliberations proved largely unrewarding.

Over the years I had kept in regular touch with Keith Young, whose business interests ran from IT to publishing. One morning he called to invite me to lunch at the RAC Club. I was, as usual, a little early and after waiting for nearly 20 minutes began to wonder whether wires had got crossed, or there had been confusion about dates. After a further few minutes he came bounding into the Club and told me he didn't have time for lunch but if I'd join him in the car, which was parked outside, he'd tell me what he wanted to discuss. I got into his Range Rover and he apologised once again for cancelling lunch and, as he drove, he asked whether I was familiar with L'Equipe or Gazzetta dello Sport.

I knew the former and we discussed the important role it played in giving the French sports' enthusiast unrivalled in depth coverage of the world of sport. Keith then told me he intended to launch a similar paper in the UK – to be called Sport First. We were now at a standstill in a bad traffic jam in Tottenham Court Road. Suddenly Keith looked at his watch and said 'I'm very late for a meeting in Gower Street, can you park the car somewhere nearby for two hours, leave the key on top of the wheel and ring my mobile to tell me where I can find it – I'll call you as soon as the meeting is over.' He then jumped out of the car and disappeared at speed down a side road whilst I slid over into the driving seat, found a parking meter and left the car in Whitfield Street. All this took place in little more than 10 minutes. He called me later and asked if we could meet the following morning at his office in Great College Street.

Keith was making plans to launch Sport First initially as a Sunday paper and, if successful, to then introduce a Saturday edition and perhaps even one mid week. He planned to kick start the project with his own money but intended to seek additional external finance. He wanted me to help with business planning and marketing as well as fundraising. Over the next few weeks we went to see a number of institutions including a flying visit to Lisbon to seek funds from a Portuguese Sports magazine owner. Meanwhile work was progressing on recruiting a production and editorial team and preparing a Business Plan. I also arranged presentations from a number of ad. agencies who had shown interest in working for the paper. After months of planning the first edition appeared and, as expected, it created considerable impact. In an era before the media had separate Sports Sections it provided superb coverage of a vast number of sports, sports personalities and results. At first it was a great success and soon a Saturday edition preceded Sunday's, but the press started to fight back and the first of the separate Sports Sections were soon on their way. Keith tried to secure additional funding to improve the content and marketing, but sadly it eventually succumbed to competition from the Newspaper Groups with much deeper pockets. However, Keith does have the satisfaction of having shaken up sports coverage in the press and being a catalyst for the now universal and highly popular Sports Sections.

My ex PA, Jane Sowerby nee Fernback, helped me from time to time with ad hoc assignments. Now her children were growing up, she was doing freelance work for Parker Harris, the visual arts consultancy, who created bespoke arts' sponsorship projects. Jane called to enquire whether I would be prepared to give them advice on business development. As a result, I had a brief and interesting relationship with Emma Parker and Penny Harris who owned the consultancy. Having become involved, I enjoyed attending and occasionally purchased paintings from some of the events they organised. These took place at the RCA, the Jerwood Centre and the Mall Galleries, where sponsors staged such competitions as ING's Discerning Eye, the Sunday Times Watercolour Exhibition and the Jerwood Prize. On one occasion, with their help and that of Keith Young, we also organised a highly successful evening at the Mall Galleries which raised funds for a very worthy woman's charity.

I was continuing to receive details of investment opportunities, most of which had little commercial appeal. One did, however, catch my eye – Wineworld or Vinopolis – a plan to convert a network of lofty arches under the railway lines near London Bridge into a restaurant, wine bar, conference complex and regional wine tasting experience for tourists. The plan was very ambitious and the total investment quite sizeable but I took a very modest stake and was asked to act as a marketing consultant for the launch. Over the years, Vinopolis has been a successful venue for product launches and sales conferences and its bar and restaurant have been highly popular destinations, but its gearing unfortunately diminished its capacity to achieve profitable growth so I exited. Another project that seemed a good idea at the time.

12

Thoburns

I had known Anna Mei Chadwick, an art dealer and a good friend of Bernard Anscomb, for some years. She called me one morning to ask if I would join her for dinner at Montpeliano with another of her friends, Richard Thoburn. She mentioned that Richard had joined CBC as a media planner shortly after I left to set up Valin Pollen and would be interested to meet me. We had a very enjoyable dinner and a few days later Richard asked me whether I would become a consultant to his company – Thoburns – which, like VPL, handles financial and corporate communications for many major UK and international companies. Richard and I got on well at dinner and I was very happy to agree. He subsequently invited me to become a shareholder and I was delighted to be given the chance to make such a good investment.

Not long after I became a consultant to Thoburns, an interesting opportunity presented itself through one of Richard Thoburn's contacts in Nigeria. The Government had decided to embark upon a programme to Privatise its State owned corporations. They proposed to commence with NITEL and were seeking a communications consultancy in London to advise them on a marketing campaign directed at both institutions and private investors. Dewe Rogerson and Hill & Knowlton had also been invited to pitch which, given Thoburns lack of privatisation experience, convinced us we probably needed to strengthen the team. I called another ex VPI colleague, Chris Matthews, now Chief Executive of Hogarth PR and he and a fellow director, Nick Denton, who had shared a flat with Richard some years previously, agreed to become part of the presentation team. This project was not without complications, because the brief also entailed the development of an educational style programme to encourage wider share ownership among a public who knew very little about investment. We were extremely pleased when we heard that our ideas had been well received and Thoburns had been awarded the project. In the event it proved to be an extremely challenging assignment, with very little profit, but it was good to beat two other consultancies that had considerable privatisation experience and also somewhat higher PR profiles.

Although I hadn't invested in a start up business for a couple of years, at around this time a friend suggested I might take a look at sparesFinder, an early stage company which, among other services, helped its clients to reduce supply costs, lower their need for working capital and also check which companies within a Group might be holding urgently required spares. I decided to invest and still have a small stake in an interesting niche business which has grown steadily over the years and now has clients in over 90 countries – but has yet to lay a Golden Egg.

One of Richard Thoburn's close friends, Ken Tonkin, owned a company, Masterplug, which manufactured small electrical products. Ken had been trying to sell the company for some time but the offers he had received were falling short of his target. I offered to try to help and Ken and I subsequently embarked upon a series of meetings with Private Equity specialists and other possible purchasers. Following a conversation with David Gyle-Thompson about Masterplug, David suggested it might be worth talking to Will Hobhouse, amongst whose other business interests was Ryness, the electrical products retailer. After I had given Will some background information about the company and made an introduction, Will and Ken spent some weeks in negotiation. Eventually after occasional personal interventions in order to sustain the momentum, a deal was finally agreed. While still falling a little short of Ken's ideal target it was, nonetheless, much better than any previous offer.

It had been quite some time since I had considered undertaking a property refurbishment project. However, I was offered two adjoining flats on the fourth floor above Emporio Armani in Brompton Road – an attractive central location. The project itself was reasonably straightforward and I made sure it was completed on time. However, as a result of wrangling between the Residents' Committee and the Managing Agents, a long planned programme to modernise the lobby area and improve its appearance was constantly delayed. This held up the sale of the flats for some months and when they were finally sold I decided I wouldn't invest in property again. Probably a poor decision in the light of escalating prices in the last 10 years.

As a result of a friendship with Martyn Kebbell, the Chairman of Maxwell Stamp, Richard Thoburn had for some years been one of the economic consultancy's shareholders. Maxwell Stamp had an excellent reputation for its work in over 100 countries on behalf of such organisations as the World Bank, the IMF and DfID and is a major player in the Overseas Aid sector. Richard mentioned that an opportunity had arisen to acquire a small stake in the company and, recognising that over time it could possibly evolve into a higher revenue earning management and economic consultancy, I felt the investment offered great potential. Whilst it is an extremely solid business, its senior management appears to be somewhat reluctant to recruit resourceful and highly motivated younger directors with the energy to accelerate the pace of profitable growth. As a result, although widely respected, it has not progressed as rapidly as I had originally hoped.

As a general recruitment principle I have always subscribed to the view that wherever and whenever possible one should hire people whose skills and abilities are superior to one's own. This is a path to greater excellence and a sound basis upon which to build any business whatever its size. I also believe the converse, where A's hire B's and they in turn hire C's, simply to avoid challenges from juniors who may show them to have shortcomings, is a recipe for a slow and lingering demise.

* * * *

Thoburns owned a freehold building in Hat & Mitre Court which, as a result of expansion, it had now outgrown. After a fairly lengthy search in the Clerkenwell area, Richard Thoburn eventually found another excellent building in Britton Street that looked ideal. I went round it with him and thought it had great potential – it even had scope for an additional floor. He decided to purchase it and after some essential decoration and minor structural changes it was finally ready for occupation and Richard and his colleagues moved in.

One Sunday morning, Richard called and asked me to join him for coffee with Nicola Davidson, the head of communications at Mittal Steel. I had met Nicola on a number of social occasions since, as well as being one of Thoburn's clients, she was a friend of John Barretto's son. She told us in confidence that Mittal might make an unsolicited bid for an unnamed company and in view of my past takeover battle experience wanted to discuss the potential PR implications. I asked who would be acting as the company's investment advisers – she mentioned Goldman Sachs. In view of the bid's significance I emphasised the importance of the highest quality investor relations and financial PR advice and suggested she should retain Angus Maitland, who she already knew. Shortly after the meeting she called Angus, who was on a sailing holiday in the Caribbean, to enlist his help. Not for the first time his holiday plans were curtailed. The next morning Mittal announced a bid for Luxembourg based Arcelor. After a tough and at times extremely hard fought battle, Arcelor finally accepted Mittal's terms which led to further entirely logical consolidation in the steel industry.

For quite some time, I had toyed with the idea of writing a novel and made one or two false starts. I finally decided to try again and, to ensure wholehearted commitment, set a deadline by which date it was to be finished. I tried to make a point of writing each day, but just before it was due to be finished, I realised I had very little time left. As with all deadlines, it focused the mind wonderfully and it was completed with a day to spare. It was called 'Echoes of a Past' and was based very loosely on some of my father's wartime experiences. To keep below the radar I used a pseudonym – sales suggest I should not repeat the exercise, although I enjoyed writing it at the time.

Richard Thoburn and I frequently discussed his plans for expanding Thoburns and the desirability of acquiring a public relations consultancy. After an extensive assessment of some of the potential candidates, he began discussions with Greentarget, a PR company with a particular strength in the financial services sector. Negotiations proved fruitful and in 2011 he acquired the company which then had to undergo some essential restructuring, largely as a result of unproductive costs associated with its underperforming design business. It is currently flourishing and as a result of Richard's direction and enthusiastic support, now has a strong team of bright, professional and highly motivated consultants.

Over the years, I have contributed to a number of interesting and challenging client and business assignments. Frequently this input has been on behalf of Thoburns' Spanish clients who particularly value the advice of a City based communications consultancy. Companies such as FCC and Repsol appointed Thoburns to help raise their profile among opinion formers, international institutional investors and the financial media that inform them – audiences with which I have long been familiar.

An especially important long term relationship has been developed with Caixabank, the largest bank in Spain which, as a result of its excellence in digital banking, is one of the most technologically advanced banks in the world. Because of its domestic focus, international media have hitherto tended to overlook many areas where the bank excels. To counteract this, and to raise its international profile, the bank has drawn on a range of services from both Thoburns and Greentarget who have worked closely together to devise an imaginative programme to enhance the bank's global reputation. Caixabank has a less well known but long established philanthropic tradition going back to the start of the last century. Richard and I have enjoyed numerous far ranging discussions whilst planning strategies designed to create wider recognition for this highly unusual and hugely impressive institution.

Richard has a reputation for being a very generous and thoughtful host, arranging immensely enjoyable lunch parties at Wimbledon and Henley and also evening events at the Goldsmith's Centre. These have been greatly appreciated by his guests who have invariably commented upon his legendary hospitality, with considerable gratitude. One particularly interesting event took place at the Centre when Roger Bootle, Chairman of Capital Economics, who had previously led a team which won the £250,000 Wolfson Economics Prize, talked very knowledgeably and persuasively about the most practical way to dismantle the Euro. I suspect many members of the EU would be delighted to be given the opportunity to exit gracefully by adopting his formula, but sadly they lack the political will and courage to push for it.

Thoburns place great emphasis on the quality of their strategic thinking and Richard recently invited me to join an Advisory Board whose other members are Shaukat Aziz, a former Prime Minister of Pakistan and Executive Vice President of Citibank, and Roger Bootle. When required, our role is to reinforce Thoburn's ability to offer clients well informed advice across a wide range of business, political and economic issues.

During this time and despite mixed success, I have still continued to back young entrepreneurs and their businesses, particularly those run by determined and creative women. One such was LuxFix, an online fashion retailer, led by Alice Hastings-Bass and Rebecca Glenapp, which offers clothing and accessories from a range of high quality British designers. Modelled on the successful Net a Porter and ASOS operations, they are winning an increasing number of clients who appreciate both style and value in women's wear and who, in common with a growing group of professional women, regularly shop online because of pressure on their time.

More recently, another impressive young woman, Harriot Pleydell–Bouverie, responded enthusiastically to the Dragons after they expressed interest in backing her Mallow & Marsh business on TV's Dragons' Den. However, she turned them down when they sought a larger share of equity for a smaller investment than she was seeking. I had been in touch with her a few weeks earlier to discuss investing in her business, but at that time she did not to require any additional finance. Now, having rejected the Dragons, with both charm and firmness, she was keen to talk. Once again I acquired a small stake and her progress to date has greatly exceeded expectations, with her range of products already to be found in all Starbucks' outlets, in Sainsbury's and in BP service stations. Harriot has the potential to be a great success and her ambitious growth projections suggest an exceptionally bright future for the business.

As part of his programme of hosting interesting evening events at the Goldsmith's Centre, Richard Thoburn arranged another particularly topical discussion a few weeks before the Referendum vote on 23 June. Richard chaired a panel comprising Roger Bootle, Douglas Carswell, UKIP's MP and the author, Frederick Forsyth. Each of the speakers made a compelling case for Brexit and, although many of the audience already appeared to be Brexit supporters, it was apparent that some of the waverers were ready to be swayed by the conviction of the speakers' powerful oratory.

I have now had a thoroughly enjoyable and very stimulating consultancy relationship with Richard for nearly 15 years. During that time we have discussed many issues, mostly business, sometimes political, but occasionally personal, of which many relate to his very deep commitment to animal welfare. He has for many years supported an animal Rescue Charity in Kent and has been especially active in rescuing dogs from brutal conditions in Romania. He recently launched Burnie's Foundation, named after his West Highland terrier, which will be devoted to the care and welfare of sick and frail animals. Richard has just sold his building in Britton Street to provide funds to acquire a property where animals can be properly cared for. This is a considerable personal commitment and an immensely worthwhile undertaking and I wish him every success with the Foundation's ambitious future plans. He is a remarkable and wholly altruistic individual.

* * * *

Not As Planned

13

Some Final Thoughts

.

'Never give up. Today is hard, tomorrow will be worse, but the day after tomorrow will be sunshine'
Jack Ma, Alibaba

I particularly like this quote, which to me, in many ways, encapsulates the essence of business life in all its ramifications. It has certainly lifted my spirits on a number of occasions when facing unwelcome problems. One can sometimes feel overexposed to seemingly trite business aphorisms, but I think they can also be a helpful source of inspiration, especially when the going gets tough, as all too often is the case.

I seem to have had a fair share of setbacks in life, many of which my friends and colleagues have considered quite extraordinary. However, I believe that being tested by having to face diverse challenges, generally builds greater resilience and ultimately the ability to cope more philosophically with whatever may yet be in store.

As a result, I tend to be fairly relaxed about unexpected events and am a great believer in 'playing the game in front of you'. When the pressure is on, there's a temptation to focus on peripheral trivia, or prevaricate endlessly, rather than tackle unpalatable problems. Better by far to deal with them immediately.

* * * *

I mentioned earlier the importance of hiring people better then yourself – I think it was David Ogilvy who added 'and then leave them to get on with it' – simply wonderful advice.

Most businesses are focused on building strong and enduring relationships with customers in order to guarantee success. I would venture to suggest that one should invest in and build equally strong relationships with one's employees, at every level, and ensure they are fully motivated and appropriately rewarded. They are the core of your business and each and every one should be a first-class ambassador for it. It's remarkable what can be achieved with enthusiastic people who share the same vision and the conviction they are the best in their field.

I think we were very fortunate within Valin Pollen in having many such individuals. Each and every one strived for excellence and there was a total commitment to winning Gold medals. All the work that is put into a new client presentation is completely fruitless unless one wins the business. Silver and Bronze are for those who don't mind their work and ideas being read and copied by the competitor who wins the assignment. We worked extremely hard to try to ensure this never happened and one year won 43 out of 47 presentations. Outstanding people, not wanting to be ordinary, but extraordinary, combined with painstaking research and strong, original ideas virtually guarantee success when in competition, in any field of endeavour.

There was great esprit de corps in Valin Pollen, which has continued throughout the years. Stuart Fenwick maintains and regularly updates records of the whereabouts of VP alumni, many of whom are in regular contact with each other. Every three or four years, since the company's demise, there has been a VP Reunion, normally attended by 50 or 60 people. Even after 25 years, their genuine pleasure in reminiscing about the years they spent together is extraordinarily gratifying, and the oft heard sentiment that they were 'the best and happiest years of my career' is immensely touching.

Over the years, a considerable number of them have gone on to build their own successful businesses in the communications industry – perhaps a testimony to some of the experience gained during their VPI years?

In today's fast changing communications environment, one cannot fail to acknowledge a debt to Sir Tim Berners Lee and his extraordinary invention, the World Wide Web. For many it has already had a dramatic impact on the way they communicate person to person, but the jury is probably still out on its likely impact on the future of the communications industry and particularly print media. An especially interesting challenge for even the most fleet footed, constantly evolving businesses as they are forced to adapt even more rapidly to disruptive innovation.

* * * *

Now, in conclusion I would like to say a particular 'thank you' to Richard Pollen, Michael Horstead and especially Angus Maitland for the part they played in these events so many years ago and without whom much of what we achieved would have been impossible.

My thanks also to Richard Thoburn for the many interesting, stimulating and enjoyable years since then, during which I have been a consultant to his company.

And finally a few personal words to Gitta and Claire, whose lives were all too often subjugated to my ambitions. One hears increasingly today of the Work – Life balance. For most of my life there was little else but work. I was committed to the accomplishment of goals and, as a result, my wife and daughter took a back seat even though I believed what I was doing was also for their benefit.

Despite an almost obsessive commitment to the work ethic, I eventually realised I had to make changes in my life and would like to put on record my gratitude to Angus Maitland for making that possible. Gitta and

Some Final Thoughts

I, although having very strong personalities, have at last found a modus operandi that suits our individual temperaments. I would like to thank her for her patience, support and loyalty over so many years.

Regrettably, my daughter Claire has not had an easy life. She has been immensely strong in coping with her ongoing battles and I salute her courage and determination in confronting her many setbacks. I hope, for her, there will be plenty of sunshine in the years ahead.

And finally, what of me. Well, at least I never had to think about an exit strategy. Maybe I should consider slowing down, but I don't think that would suit me. I'm quite impatient and somewhat driven in my approach to life – always looking for the next interesting opportunity or challenge.

Perhaps with that thought in mind, these recollections might better have been titled – What Next?

THE VPI GROUP - A GLOSSARY

VPI - Valin Pollen International,
the publicly quoted parent of the Group

VPL - Valin Pollen Ltd., the UK financial
and corporate communications company

CVP - Carter Valin Pollen, the Group's UK
and US investor relations consultancy

MWB - McAvoy Wreford Bayley,
the UK PR consultancy

VPT&K - VPI's Dutch subsidiary, formed
when it acquired Thomas & Kleyn in 1985

HRH CONSENSUS - Formed when Consensus
Research merged with HRH International

APT - APT Photoset, acquired by VPI in 1985

FALCON – Falcon Designs,
finished artwork and design studio

TCO – The Carter Organization, the New York
proxy solicitation, investor relations and stock
surveillance specialist, acquired by VPI in 1987

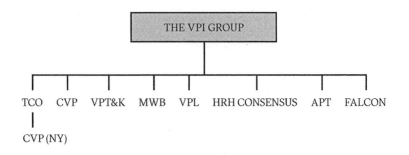